Now, Barabbas

NOW, BARABBAS

William Jovanovich

Harper & Row, Publishers
New York, Evanston,
and London

First Edition

Library of Congress
Catalog Card Number: 64:19552
Designed by The Etheredges
G–O

To my Mother
Hedviga Jovanovich

Contents

Contents

Preface

During the course of writing this book I began to understand, with surprising discomfort, that an author's antagonism toward his publisher can at times be both natural
and necessary. Soon after a contract was signed between
us, Harper's editors set about asking me questions. Did I
intend to treat of bookselling customs, of international
trade, of this and of that? Was there a unifying theme in
the essays? In response, I found myself becoming noncom-
mittal, then evasive, and finally silent. At last, they asked
politely when the manuscript would be delivered. When
indeed! To keep a schedule in writing is an inhuman
ordeal: one is asked to suffer—and to yield to—his own
inadequacies *on time*. Fortunately, now that the work is
done, my conversion to an author's point of view has been
arrested. I have regained the saving and self-serving per-
spective of a publisher, the proof of which is that I do not
intend to ask Harper & Row why they have so meagerly

announced the publication of my book, nor why they have failed to send advertising letters to those countless thousands of readers who, were they merely informed, would buy. I know the answers to such complaints. I have given them myself too often not to recognize that they are regrettably reasonable, and always unsatisfying.

The eleven parts of this volume all deal with the publishing of books and in consequence they touch, however obliquely, on the nature of writing and reading and learning. Only one part is directly personal, that titled "A Vision of Good and Evil: Part Two," which describes my relations with the writer and Yugoslav political leader Milovan Djilas. I have chosen to include it here because it is, I think, a dramatic revelation of the plight of a writer who is important to our time. It suggests, moreover, the personal commitment a publisher can make to writers and readers alike. Otherwise, I have not attempted to describe or explain my own experiences as a publisher and, thereby, have tried to escape a common fallacy in my profession, which is the prideful assumption that publishers are as much the initiators as the purveyors of good works. Yet there is another kind of pride that I trust emerges from this book: my conviction that publishing is one of the most civilized of worldly pursuits.

W. J.

March 17, 1964
Briarcliff Manor

"Now Barabbas was a publisher."

—LORD BYRON

Now, Barabbas

Lord Byron was never properly put to rest; the disputes in his life were banked, and even now they glow fitfully. Byron himself was less tempestuous than the world chooses to believe—he possessed perfect manners and was, whilst in health, a tolerant companion—yet it was his misfortune to arouse in others an extravagance of feeling. Among these others was his publisher, John Murray. On the subject of publishers Byron is best remembered for his remark "now Barabbas was a publisher," but he gave to Murray his friendship and the care of his considerable literary properties. How Murray dealt with one of these properties on Byron's death is a tale that suggests, with a nicely fashioned irony, the propensities of publishers.

The tale is told by Doris Langley Moore, a scholar who in her search for Byron's papers has affirmed the power of his charm and the persistence of its effects.

"I am," Mrs. Moore writes, "perhaps the only woman to whom nothing but pleasure has come from having loved that poet . . . how odd, how perfectly incredible, I should have thought it when, as an adolescent girl, I first started on my Byron quest, had I been told that the greatest, most exciting, most moving experience it would bring me was to take place when I was a woman of fifty-four!" The quest—such romantic terms are invoked by Byron—took Mrs. Moore, by a stroke of rare luck, to Judith, Baroness Wentworth, the only great-grandchild of Lord Byron and the guardian of his private papers. Lady Wentworth lived to a great age and was, in the seclusion of her eccentricity, a creator of legends. Once I talked with an English writer who had, after years of waiting for an invitation, like Mrs. Moore, gained access to Crabbet Park and was shown into a room where Lady Wentworth sat, looking, he said, like Charles II in a red wig. "Do you know my son?" she asked, and, on being told he did not, continued, "I haven't seen him in twenty years." "Has he been abroad?" asked the writer, it itself, given the circumstance, a deliciously English question. "No, he's in England," said Lady Wentworth. "The last time I saw him was in this very room, standing as you do; in one pocket he had a pistol and in the other a copy of Aquinas, and he threatened me with both."

But I digress from Mrs. Moore's account of the burning of Byron's memoirs, which is briefly this: Byron wrote his memoirs during the time between 1818 and 1821. He generously gave the manuscript of some four hundred pages to Thomas Moore, the Irish poet who was then as always beset by debts, with approval to Moore to assign it to John Murray for the sum of two thousand guineas, providing that the memoirs would not be published during Byron's lifetime. On his death in 1824, some of Byron's friends, with the curious and altogether self-defeating aid of John Murray, were seized by an urgent desire to destroy the manuscript in order to spare Lady Byron and Augusta Leigh, Byron's half-sister, from its supposedly damaging revelations. Quarreling with one another, each driven by a peculiar fervor, six gentlemen gathered in Murray's drawing room in Albemarle Street. The memoirs had been read by only two of this number, Moore and one other—though not Murray, in whose safe the manuscript had lain for almost three years. Of those persons who had read the manuscript—there were several not present in Albemarle Street—not one, to our present knowledge, found it to be scandalous. Yet the meeting proceeded to its lunatic end.

The end came once Murray had summoned his son and heir, a boy of sixteen, to witness the occasion. What was surely a notable work of literature was put, sheaf upon sheaf, into the flames. Moore, who had weakly protested, was now turned upon by some of the others with the accusatory reminder that Murray, though a "tradesman," had acted like a gentleman in giving up the manuscript for which he had paid so dearly. Moore was then, incredibly, prevailed upon to repay Murray the two thousand guineas *together with interest and postal charges.* Byron's biographer finishes her story with this last turn of the screw: "Still unsated, Hobhouse asked him [Moore] before they dispersed to own 'that Murray had acted perfectly well and honourably in the business,' to which Moore retorted, with a laugh that must have been rather a wry one, that he was like the Irishman who, when a judge inquired if he had anything to say why sentence of death should not be passed upon him, exclaimed 'Oh nothing, except by Jasus you've settled it all very nicely amongst you.' "

Certain propensities of publishers, like homely morals, that we may draw from this tale are obvious. Despite a strong sense of tradition and family pride (publishers even now call their firms "houses"), Murray was regarded, and indeed so identified himself, as a "tradesman." In our own day the publishing of books for the general public is particularly called "the trade." Yet like publishers before him, and after, Murray was something more and something less than a tradesman. He was the businessman *manqué.* Conceive of paying the equivalent of ten thousand guineas (or thirty thousand dollars) in today's currency for a book you might not be allowed to publish for forty years (Byron was but thirty-two years of age when Murray

paid over the sum), by which time the author might well
have fallen into public neglect. Conceive, too, of the
buyer's not seeing the property before its purchase, nor
examining it once he gained its possession. Surely, such
are the acts of a gambler, or a friend, but not of a sensible
businessman. Murray, however, was most successful. He
did publish Byron's works, and among them *Childe
Harold,* Cantos One and Two of which comprised the
best-selling volume of poetry in modern times (one hundred and forty-six years later, the seventh head of the
house, John Grey Murray, published John Betjeman's
Collected Poems and, on discovering that it was selling at
the rate of one thousand copies a week, announced that it
was the firm's *second* most popular work of poetry).
Moreover, we have seen that John Murray was able to
recover his investment from Moore, who inevitably must
be a poet. It is typical, too, that Murray, having made the
quixotic gesture of destroying his own property, should
recoup not only his capital investment but also his overhead in the form of "interest and postal charges." Somerset
Maugham concludes in one of his short stories that in this
life it is better to be lucky than skillful. Every publisher
secretly believes it.

Not everyone dwells gently on the contradictions in
a publisher's role. In *The Observer,* the writer "Pendennis"
declares that book publishers are egotistical and notori-
ously disloyal to one another. The first charge is likely

true, for most publishers are men of strong prejudices (and small scholarship), but the second charge is irrelevant and incompetent. There is no good reason why publishers should be loyal to each other: it is important that they be loyal to their authors. To do this is in itself difficult enough, for too soon does egotism intrude and the publisher finds himself minding his own reputation rather than the author's. The story of one notable publisher's life turns out to be, relentlessly and humorlessly, a tale told in numbers, a shilling lost, a pound gained, an author lost, an author found. Whether or not this criticism is fair, the making of it is altogether natural, for publishers, like actors, are devoted to gossip and to the habit of rating their peers. The same conversations are repeated in London and Paris and Milan as in New York: "Of course, Grubkins is very successful but he simply isn't a *publisher;* on the other hand, poor Narcisski is going broke—too bad, he's a serious publisher but he's just not a businessman." The ideal publisher, it would seem, should be practical but not too much so, as Alfred North Whitehead once suggested of college presidents. When Whitehead was told that James Bryant Conant had succeeded the venerable Mr. Lowell as president of Harvard he appeared not to recognize the name, and when he was told further that Conant was a biochemist he was visibly surprised. "After all," said his informant, "President Eliot was a chemist."

"I know," said Whitehead, "but he wasn't a very good one, was he?"

It is no doubt because the publisher can at once be regarded as a scoundrel by his authors and as an idealist by his bankers that he suffers a certain ambiguity over his own identity. Fredric Warburg calls his autobiography *An Occupation for Gentlemen* and Sir Stanley Unwin calls his *The Truth About a Publisher,* as if each needed to exorcise a particular doubt about his profession. Yet, things change, and perhaps the publisher's identity, no less than his dilemma, will not long remain private. Millionaires have of late discovered that book publishing can be stimulating, especially if the mixture is at least four parts textbooks to one part literature. Articles on books now appear in *Fortune* and *The Wall Street Journal.* And publishing-stock prospectuses are to be found on the tables of brokers everywhere. Now, Barabbas.

Of publishers it may be said that like the English as a race they are incapable of philosophy. They deal in particulars and adhere easily to Sydney Smith's dictum that one should take short views, hope for the best, and trust God. Their days are filled with royalty rates, accounts and discounts, last printings and first remainders, and it is reasonable to ask even of Malraux or Faulkner how many copies of his previous book were sold. The usual general questions tend, on the other hand, either to bore them or to embarrass them. Has television diminished book reading? Why are there no great editors any more, or, for that matter, no great writers any more? Do you read fast? Are book clubs good for the common people? The answer to all these questions, incidentally, is no.

There are more acute questions and larger ideas, and every publisher soon or late reflects on his duty. Publishing is, I think, a primarily civilizing enterprise and like orderly government it is central to a humanistic society. Its great import lies in the maintenance of freedom. This, the finest propensity of publishing, I propose to deal with briefly.

It is a mistake, surely, to presume that intellectual freedom in this age is advanced by the same degree as are science and technology. Progress is never absolute and most often it is not even relative: some things were done better before. There is, in fact, less diversity of serious opinion and there are fewer statements showing original style and thought in the American press today than in the press of a half-century ago. Our talents have not declined but our candor has. It is hard to conceive of H. L. Mencken or Lincoln Steffens writing now with the free-swinging iconoclasm they employed in their day. Even the penny press, which enjoys the leeway we give to gaucherie, is not so bold as it once was. Could Robert Green Ingersoll dispute the promises of an afterlife in next Sunday's supplement? I think not. The press has found new pieties.

From its timidity not only does vigorous expression suffer but also the public taste, for what passes as forthrightness in today's journalism is likely to be mere vulgarity, as in the writing of Robert Ruark. Style, after all, is not alone how one says things, but how one conceives them.

Although books are not the most immediately powerful form of expression in our society, they comprise the freest form. Neither the press nor radio and television is so *sure* in the enlargement and defense of intellectual liberty. It may be argued *extenuare* that books, unlike newspapers, are made safe from popular pressures by being addressed to the few; that the buyer of books exercises an individual choice—tempered by a high price—whereas the newspaper subscriber receives issue after issue on trust and without prior examination or reviewal. Is this, finally, relevant? Intellectual freedom is not, in the long view, measured by readers, but by writers. An idea of value develops its own motive power and will move through many minds.

The publisher may, then, look beyond the particulars of his art and enterprise, beyond the need to keep honest with his authors, to keep solvent with his creditors and if not solvent at least cheerful. He may look to his duty, which is to be unafraid, trust in his own taste, and respect genius. Professor Whitehead in his *Dialogues* said that "the vitality of thought is in adventure. *Ideas won't keep*. Something must be done about them." A publisher is one of those men in a humane society whose public trust it is to do something about ideas. We live in a prosaic age and can be reminded that ideas, to bear value, need not be phrased in a socially pragmatic form. Fiction and poetry and criticism, because they are the higher art, yield more lasting ideas on the human condition than do most disquisitions on society. There is not much pleasure, though there may be profit, in selling a pot of message. The publishing of tracts can be a dreary business unless one has a passionate impatience with the future and cannot believe, with Emerson, that it is best to keep cool for all will be one a hundred years hence.

To do something about other people's ideas, it will be seen, requires some part of prescience, of taste, and of courage, and the last is hardest to come by. If the publisher's best duty is his defense of free expression, then his gravest threat is censorship. It persists, being the ready tool of governments, churches, and armies. Censorship is not always official (I am puzzled by the repeated use of the pejorative phrase "self-appointed censor." Is the volunteer censor really more reprehensible than the certified one?), but it always depends on the exercise of power. The censor makes use of, and sees dangers in, numbers. A nude in a museum is seen by few, in a magazine by many; the first is proper, the second a peril. A novel containing rude words is worse for being sold at fifty cents than at five dollars. Those who cannot pay the price are allowed less. Numbers, too, are the source of the censor's power, his last and best threat being to reduce the publisher's sales. For the general publisher, there is the threat that censorship will discourage him from issuing certain books if there is no chance of their being variously reviewed; and, even more serious, there is the threat that his publishing certain general books will result in a boycott of his textbooks—though they are wholly unrelated—in schools and colleges. The struggle continues, and if the censors will not quit (sometimes they do: a century ago, the King of Saxony's Board of Censors resigned on the grounds that the nature of their job was dishonorable), neither shall the publishers. One cannot, in favor of the truth, avoid giving offense to fortune, but one should avoid giving hostages to it.

It is, no doubt, all too easy to exalt the publisher's art and enterprise. Look with guilt, says the critic, on the thousand footling books issued each year that were not in the first instance worth printing. Literature is not, in fact, cheapened by quantity, and one great book overshadows a thousand poor ones. Yet there *are* too many books published. The publisher was in the beginning of time visited by two curses: one, that for every subject, however dreary, there must be a reader; and two, that there is no accounting for people's tastes. He is cursed but he may also be blessed, for his is the chance to recognize in today's typescript a classic of tomorrow's library; and if he should put his money on many numbers in order to win with one, surely he will be forgiven his recklessness.

And if he be forgiven, how shall he be rewarded? His efforts are not always profitable, for his propensities, like those of John Murray, are often narrow, sometimes quixotic and even outrageous. Now and again he meets with genius, and to have been Lord Byron's friend would serve a man a lifetime. Perhaps, after all, his reward comes in the last hour. An early nineteenth-century economist with the delightful and improbable name of Nassau Senior once proved to his own satisfaction that only in the last hour that a mill or shop ran was any profit to be made. Up to then, owing to the high costs of materials and overhead and depreciation, no profit was forthcoming, and if the laborer demanded that his workday be cut from twelve to eleven hours, the enterprise would be ruined. So it may be with publishing. The effort is dear, the results are uncertain, and the eye of eternity dims, but it shall all have been worthwhile if in the last hour the publisher holds in his hand that most singular of promises: a good book.

Variety in a Little Room

It is a fine precept, however infrequently practiced, that a publisher should commit himself only to those books that engage him most seriously and thus confine his excesses to his interests. This suggests that there are sound personal reasons for the existence of many different kinds of publishing, and it may help to explain why publishing does not tend to follow a uniform procedure. Indeed, it borrows little from the precision and dispatch that Americans have perfected in the making and marketing of mass-produced articles. The uniqueness of a book, any book, argues against the refinement of those skills based on repetition of effort. It is for this reason I am not overly dismayed that my colleagues and I seem to approach each book as if we had never made one before. (There may be another, and Rousseauesque, explanation for our artless behavior. Of Martinique natives it used to be said that within a fortnight they could progressively *forget* how to operate a simple machine.)

Book publishing is not in any event large enough to become mechanized. Its modest size as an industry—at least in the days before the advent of publishing shares on the stock market—has been for some reason a source of wonder. It has been said that in dollar volume more dog food is sold yearly than textbooks, and what this proves other than that dogs eat more than they read I am not sure; or again, it is said that, lamentably, more money is spent on caskets than on general trade books, a comparison that can have no meaning unless they are both regarded as repositories of dead matter. It can be stated simply, without the melodrama of such statistics, that book publishing is not a large industry nor likely to become one. It employs thousands of people, not hundreds of thousands, and not one firm in the United States has yet qualified, on the sale of books alone, for inclusion in the annual grand honors list of *Fortune*'s five hundred largest corporations. Yet it has, to mix Marlowe with Shakespeare, an infinite variety in a little room. During the mid-1960's there are about twenty-five thousand titles published annually in the United States, and there are more than one hundred and seventy thousand titles in print. These are books of all dimensions made for all intents and purposes, books printed in runs as great as a quarter-million copies or as small as two hundred, books sold for a quarter and for five hundred dollars, books that will scarcely be remembered, save for their authors' pride and their publishers' regret, and books that are indestructible.

But the plethora of publishing can hold small interest unless one has some notion of the descriptions that identify different kinds of publishing. Some of these definitions are logical and obvious, others are parochial and somewhat unreliable, as for example the American term "trade" that is applied to books which in England are more sensibly called "general books." Trade books can be anything. Indeed, what defines them is their very generality: these are volumes of common interest stocked in bookstores to attract a wide public—works of fiction, biography, history, poetry, criticism, travel, children's literature, and so forth. Some books that are more specialized but are nonetheless sold through regular trade channels, notably bookstores, are also called trade titles, such as dictionaries, industrial handbooks, business guides, cookbooks, scientific monographs, and atlases.

Textbooks present no such complications and their category is rarely mistaken (though their orthography often is—the New York City Board of Education still spells the word "text books"). They are produced for explicitly defined courses in the elementary and secondary schools and in colleges, universities, and technical institutions. Generally they follow the subject matter of a prescribed course, but it is not unknown for a trade book to become a textbook simply by being taken up by a teacher and regularly required of his students. There is, in the matter of definition, at least one complication; not all educational publishing has to do with books. Since World War II the textbook publisher has progressively found it necessary, given the nature of contemporary teaching, to issue filmstrips, laboratory manuals, classroom tests, phonograph records and tapes, and even scientific kits full of hardware.

If a salesman presents himself at your door to sell you an encyclopedia or the six-volume Sangamon Edition of Sandburg's *Lincoln,* offering credit terms as an inducement, you will have glimpsed a part of what the trade calls "subscription publishing." Door-to-door bookselling in America has chiefly to do with reference books and, among these, chiefly with encyclopedias. There is, in consequence, an indistinct line between reference publications and all other subscription books, hence it cannot be invidious to regard them jointly.

Historically, reprint publishing is allied to reference books, for it was common during the nineteenth century for reprinted editions of standard works in sets of possibly ten or twenty volumes to be sold door to door. Most reprints, which are reissues of previously published works offered at a lower price and usually in an altered format, are today in the form of paperback books. Publishers used to speak some years ago of "cheap" paperbacks and "quality" paperbacks, but this comparison was offensive

to those houses who were issuing the Koran at fifty cents
and Graham Greene at thirty-five, so today it is more
common to distinguish between "lower-priced" and
"higher-priced" reprint books.

Educational tests are a little-known form of publishing, although it is certain that few living Americans have
not used its products, which are the pamphlets and answer
sheets and cards employed by schools to measure, variously, the mental aptitudes, the interests, and the scholastic
achievements of individual students. Educational tests are
sold mainly to schools, though only rarely to colleges,
and a few are bought by industrial companies to measure
the aptitudes of employees. It is mainly these that have of
late brought test publishing to public notice, for tests have
been attacked as still another evidence of how modern
society creates the "mass mind" and fosters the "organization man," neither of which, surely, can be as prevalent
as is claimed, given the sheer number of critics who
expose them.

Now it will be seen that these five categories—trade
books, textbooks, reference and subscription books, reprints, and educational tests—are not exclusive. An encyclopedia is sold in bookstores like a trade book though it
is a reference book, and a dictionary can hardly be denied
its utility as a work of reference by being called a trade
book. One need not linger over such distinctions, for that
way lies pedantry and worse, bad temper, if one considers

that the root word is itself misused, as among some American advertising men and London hairdressers who share the barbarous habit of calling a magazine a book.

Though it is properly the desire of the literary-minded college senior to come to New York, take up residence in a publishing house and begin to entertain at lunch the likes of Saul Bellow, the plain fact is that there are only a score of good trade editorial jobs open each year. For every editor who advises the author of a novel, there are at least twenty at work on a secondary-school science textbook. Yet the cachet of trade publishing is seemingly undiminishable. Everyone has heard of Maxwell Perkins, but who knows the name of the editor of the *Dictionary of American Biography* or Paul A. Samuelson's *Economics?* (It is curious how Perkins as an editor has dominated the trade imagination and how little is said of his peers, among them Ben Huebsch, Pat Covici, and Saxe Cummins.) The disparity in jobs between trade and textbook publishing has in part to do with their relative volume of sales. While trade books comprise about two-fifths of the total dollar volume of sales from all book publishing, those particular titles that are regularly reviewed in magazines and journals—the fiction and non-fiction for adults—constitute but a tenth of the total.

While trade publishing is quite vigorous, it has long been harassed by the difficulty of reaching the public readily and inexpensively. Al Smith, when he was Governor of the State of New York, was supposed to have said, "If I wanted to buy a book where would I go?" It is not recorded that he waited for an answer. Fifty years ago the public bought books mainly from bookstores, where available in the larger towns and the cities, and otherwise from itinerant salesmen and from mail-order catalogs. During the 1920's two new vigorous means of bookselling appeared, both dependent upon the mails: book clubs and direct-mail coupon advertising. Soon after, the Great Depression took its toll of small businesses, including bookstores. The immediate effect of the Depression was to decrease within two years, from 1929 to 1931, the number of books produced by thirty-five per cent, and dollar sales by perhaps as much as fifty per cent. Yet even then, as now, publishers were attributing their problems to the unliterary impulses of Americans. In 1934 the magazine *Index* spoke of "the effect upon book sales of such competitive forms of recreation as the automobile, the radio, and moving pictures. . . ." (No doubt there has always been an unfeigned puzzlement about hard times, not unlike that of the writer, nee Roosevelt, who once told me that her family had moved to her grandfather's house at Oyster Bay after 1929 because "something seems to have happened to Daddy's money about that time.")

World War II brought a respite from the struggle to reach a greater audience of book buyers, simply because publishers were able to sell practically everything to war-workers, who had plenty of money and not much to spend it on. Book-club memberships soared and, at one point, shortly after the war, the Book-of-the-Month Club approached a million subscribers (today its membership is apparently about six hundred and fifty thousand). With the coming of peace, the trade publisher's ailments, like old friends, eventually returned one by one, and by 1950 the *number of copies* of books sold through bookstores had subsided almost to the 1929 level. Of late, however, matters have improved considerably. Not only are publishers getting better prices for their books but the volume of copies sold has increased as well, and new markets for books have been opened by the success of paperbacks, art books, and educational works of all kinds. Today the bookstore must, as before, compete against book clubs and mail-order selling and, still more recently, the "discount" department stores that sometimes use best sellers as "loss leaders" in order to lure customers into their premises. Articles sold at cost, or even below cost, are known as loss leaders. This is a strictly *retail* practice, yet it was applied incongruously to publishing in an intriguing fashion by Alfred Knopf, Jr. Mr. Knopf's firm, Atheneum, decided to spend forty thousand dollars advertising and promoting a paperback reprint edition of a book written by Governor Nelson A. Rockefeller. To the New York *Times,* which inquired about this extraordinary expenditure, Mr. Knopf put aside any implication that the Governor's political supporters were helping to subsidize the publisher; his firm, he said, was treating the book as a loss leader. The *Times* did not pursue his meaning, nor, typically, did anyone in publishing, yet he can only have meant that other authors will be lured into the premises of Atheneum on the self-ruinous promise of such extravagant treatment. Considering that Atheneum was only the reprint publisher for the Governor, and considering the Governor's presently poor chances in the race for the Presidency, I should like to believe that Mr. Knopf was punning.

The bookseller, like the publisher, is encouraged by the accelerating effects of America's economy, and both have intimations of a steady enlargement of the reading audience for general books. They can, perhaps, hope that the concept of "the luxury of consumption" will one day function for books; once consumers are surfeited with the goods that now carry social prestige they may decide that owning a modest library lends as much status as does a dishwasher. Perhaps, when that comes about, the matter of price will not seem so important as it does now. Book prices in the trade are relatively high precisely because the sale of the average trade book is low; the publisher gives high discounts to the bookseller, as well as the privilege to return unsold stock, because the bookseller's turnover is small. It is obvious that both need to sell more to sell cheaper, and if this presently offers little consolation they can at least take refuge in the patriotic reflection that capitalism works.

Not that trade publishers do not have expectations. In the United States there are more than three hundred and fifty of them who issue more than five titles a year, and their number has grown with good times. Not all of this number are engaged solely in trade publishing. Many of them spread their risks by diversifying their lists, particularly by including textbooks, which are not only more profitable to publish, dollar for dollar of sales, than trade books but also are increasing in volume at a rate more than twice that of the national economy as a whole. Demography cannot be denied. In 1963 there were 35,000,000 students in American elementary schools (grades one through eight), 12,100,000 in secondary schools, and 4,386,000 in colleges. By 1970 the total will be at least a fifth greater, with as many as 7,000,000 people enrolled in colleges alone. These are all learners, and on the other end of the log are textbooks.

Given so hopeful a prospect, it may be wondered why all publishers do not undertake to issue textbooks. The reasons are not complicated: some of them lack the interest, others lack the skill, and most of them lack the money. Textbooks require an immense investment in capital. It is quite possible—though it does indeed seem excessive—for a publisher to spend one million dollars in cash on the preparation of an elementary series of eight textbooks before selling a single copy, and as much as one hundred and fifty thousand dollars on a single high school book, or seventy-five thousand dollars on a college book on, for example, psychology or American history. The structure of the major textbook houses is built on the big book for the big course, and it is for this reason that publishers are expected to perform services for the schools (and even the colleges) that were unimagined forty years ago. To accompany a fourth-grade science book in a "basic series" the publisher either sells or donates to the schools an accompanying workbook, a teacher's manual on how to use the complex of materials, a series of filmstrips, a booklet of tests, a box of laboratory experiment cards, and a kit of simple objects for use in classroom experiments (one publisher lists in his kit a toilet tissue and an empty Coca-Cola bottle, like props in a Truman Capote story). Before this extraordinary array is actually bought, it is expected that the publisher will have sent to the school a "consultant" to demonstrate the teaching of fourth-grade science, and, of course, he will have already several times dispatched salesmen and mailed a series of advertising brochures and letters.

That the resources such publishing requires are large is plain enough, not alone in capital funds but in staff. A textbook house with annual net sales of $25,000,000 from school textbooks is likely to employ about seventy-five editors and copy editors and one hundred and twenty salesmen and sales managers, whereas a trade publisher with half that sale can manage on only a fifth as many editorial and sales people. Given the money, the skill, and the patience, a textbook publisher can make his fortune, if not necessarily his mark. To contribute seriously to education he needs a measure of daring and imagination, and these are the most precious of elements to come by. Martin Mayer in *The Schools* has demonstrated convincingly (though he has also, I suspect, mistaken the stolid unawareness of some publishers for villainy, which is to say too much against them and, indeed, for them) that American textbook houses have been slow to experiment with new approaches to learning because they seek to maintain their interests in books that are palpably inadequate. American textbook publishing is, in a paradoxical way, constricted by the very definiteness of its market. Too often the salesman refutes the editor with the argument that it is sensible and safe to offer the schools what they are already using. Reform is not to be achieved, I think, by governmental intervention or by the entry of university presses into textbook publishing, as Mayer has suggested, nor will it likely be brought about largely by smaller houses that presumably have not yet become comatose from the effects of prosperity. Rather, the need is for braver, better people to enter the larger houses and reassert what is obvious, namely that American education's chief virtue has been its flexibility and its willingness to alter its ways and means. There are simply not enough intellectually first-rate people in textbook publishing: what is regarded as clever reactionism by some critics can be more reasonably viewed as general mediocrity.

Whatever his results may be, the textbook publisher must, in any event, pay his costs from his own sales. The licensing of reprint and other subsidiary rights does not enter into textbooks at all. By now it must be known to everyone, as the favorite jeremiad in the book business, that the average trade publisher would show a loss were it not for his "other income," that is, sales of rights to paperback reprint houses, to book clubs, to foreign publishers, and, occasionally, to radio, television, magazines, and the movies. But the textbook publisher has no subsidiary rights, or rarely so. S. I. Hayakawa's *Language in Action* is one of the very few textbooks, if not the only one, to be chosen by the Book-of-the-Month Club, and it was in the nature of its origin, I suppose, that the Club issued the book in December of 1941, an improbable selling season for an author with a Japanese name.

During the nineteenth century one could buy the *Works of Channing* or *The Novels of Sir Walter Scott* from itinerant book peddlers who were the butt of contemporary theatrical humor and, later, of the good-natured satire of Finley P. Dunne's Mr. Dooley. This was an early form of subscription selling whose modern practice is given mainly to the sale of encyclopedias and children's reference series (*The World Book Encyclopedia*) and various sets of classics, including *The Great Books*. While reference-book publishing and subscription selling are closely allied, they are not, as I have already indicated, strictly coincident, especially as the immense sale of reference books in supermarkets has been added to the fairly minor distribution of these works through bookstores (the one-volume *Columbia Encyclopedia* remains the only major encyclopedia sold chiefly by booksellers).

For the general publisher no less than for the layman the distribution (and hence the publication) of encyclopedias is a strange pursuit. Their sale to householders door to door by certain techniques has drawn injunctions from the Fair Trade Commission as well as the disgust of Dr. Harvey Einbinder, whose criticism of the *Encyclopædia Britannica* has finally been issued by Grove Press. (He has an interesting story to tell about the preparation of his book and his relations with magazines and publishers, several of whom, including my own firm, turned it down for one reason or another.) Einbinder describes the merchandising devices that so many householders have suffered from: the telephone call from the local "sales manager" identifying the listener as a community leader who has been singled out to receive a special discount, the offer of various types of binding whose prices do not entirely relate to the costs of materials, the claims for current revision that are absurdly contradicted by the text in certain places, the advertisements showing small children who could not in any event read the *Encyclopædia Britannica,* but whose tender, vulnerable faces are so depicted as to make a parent feel anxious about the family's education at home, and so on. Merchandising so dominates the subscription selling of encyclopedias that one finds it indeed forbearing that no television network has yet pointed out that Newton Minow, the former head of the Federal Communications Commission, left his post to *re*-enter what could be called another vast "wasteland."

Whatever else may be said about the particular questions of how they are sold and revised, encyclopedias are certainly lucrative, according to former Senator William Benton, the chairman and (with the University of Chicago) the owner of the *Encyclopædia Britannica,* who told the Harvard Club in New York that some of his sales managers made as much as one hundred and twenty-five thousand dollars during 1958. As an industry, reference books (not counting dictionaries) exceeded $375,000,000 in net sales (that is, what the publishers received) in 1962, a new climax in a business that has grown enormously since the end of World War II. One might think that so great a market would encourage some publisher to issue a wholly new encyclopedia that had the scope and impetus of Diderot's or, more relevantly, of the great Eleventh

Edition (1910–1911) of the *Encyclopædia Britannica*. No single publication is more needed in American education than an encyclopedia whose essays are written in the individual styles of the major historians, scientists, artists, and other humanists of our day. Yet, if a publisher eschewed door-to-door selling with such a work, as he indeed ought to do, he could never make the work pay its way.

The advance of dictionaries during the past quarter-century is more encouraging, particularly since lexicographical scholarship has during this period improved on much of what appeared in earlier dictionaries. There are now a number of dictionaries that deserve respect, and so, in a sense, do their publishers, who were required to risk a very great investment in their preparation—for a new dictionary of the "college" size the investment is no less than two-thirds of a million dollars. Yet the desk dictionary of fifteen hundred pages or so remains one of the most underpriced of all books. Dictionaries share with Bibles the unhappy distinction of requiring a high cost of production but commanding only a low price in the store, as if buyers demanded that what is held indispensable should also be cheap.

If singularity and specialization are the characteristics of the reference-book publisher, then a contrast is furnished by the reprint publisher, who cultivates eclecticism. Reprint publishing is a world of its own and, it may be, a world without end. Books are one of the few products in our society that can be sold and resold without necessarily becoming secondhand. What is even more wondrous is the possibility that a book can be sold and resold to the same buyer, as must happen occasionally when a paperback reprint bears a different title from its original edition and when its cover displays scenes that are usually nonexistent in the text. Not long ago I bought a Simenon for thirty-five cents only to discover that I had six months earlier bought the original hard-cover edition. I cannot really blame anyone for this; my own firm once published Georges Simenon, and it was obviously a mistake that I had to *buy* copies of his books at all. (There are happy endings in publishing, if not in most books by Simenon, who has, I am pleased to say, rejoined our house.)

A quarter of a century ago there were substantially no cheap paperback reprints, although paperbacks are hardly new—their antecedents in the nineteenth century are many, including the dime novels of Street and Smith. During World War II, paperback books were given a great impetus when the Armed Services Editions distributed 122,500,000 copies of books on license from American publishers. The paperback-reprint market is now a huge one, exceeding 300,000,000 copies a year. It has achieved a breadth of distribution that the hard-cover publisher cannot possibly emulate. Reprints are sent through the channels of hundreds of wholesalers and more than one hundred thousand retailers, as compared with the wretchedly few bookstores that distribute hard-cover books. No more than fifteen hundred bookstores can call bookselling their chief business; possibly no more than five hundred can claim to carry a reasonably serviceable stock of backlist titles.

While paperbacks of a cheap price are found in an enormous number of outlets they nonetheless suffer, as magazines do, a rapid turnover. Each competes desperately for display space at the newsstand or drugstore, and each is held in stock only briefly, with a life cycle scarcely greater than that of a fruit fly. Because of his dependence on a broad distribution system comprised of impatient retailers, the reprint publisher is always in danger of being overstocked. A decade ago there were at one time 200,000,000 copies in warehouses and it was found necessary to destroy 60,000,000 paperbacks within a single year. Reprints have no "remainder" value (books are "remaindered" to certain jobbers who resell them at drastically reduced prices) unless they can be sold overseas for a penny or two. The hard-cover book, incidentally, declines at a slower pace through more stages of desuetude. The last stage, I have been told, though I cannot vouch for its authenticity, is almost too sad to relate: after a book has been remaindered for resale at perhaps fifty-nine cents and then nineteen cents, a publisher can, with his face averted, send a *large* book to a place in New Jersey where the middle of the text is scooped out for the insertion of a jack-in-the-box.

Not all paperbacks are treated like magazines; bookstores keep in stock practically all of the more expensive ones, like the Anchor, Vintage, Harvest, Meridian, Dolphin, and other series that for occult reasons bear either nautical or autumnal names. When Pocket Books, the pioneer of contemporary paperbacks, began in 1939, the publishers giving them reprint licenses stipulated that these twenty-five-cent books could not be sold through bookstores. Now, of course, there are paperbacks of every price in bookstores, and there are bookstores which stock nothing but paperbacks. That these books can be considered popular simply because they are cheap in price is no longer a sound premise. Higher and higher the price has gone, until it is not unusual to find paperbacks at two dollars and ninety-five cents and even three dollars and forty-five cents. In fact, the suspicion grows that one could publish the same book in hard cover and paper cover with the latter selling more copies *even at a higher price*. There is a certain fashionableness about the so-called quality paperbacks, the persistence of which has led publishers to rummage about in their backlists for any title that will sound even vaguely familiar to a college student, especially if it relates to myth, symbol, and the angst of the human condition. Yet, I confess that this is the cynicism of the "insider." One ought to guard against underestimating the genuine motive to expand taste and learning that has informed both the reading and the publishing of good books at a low price. Indeed, the most hopeful development in publishing in our time has been the proliferation of reading serious books in paperback form. Among college students alone such books have advanced education to a degree that is still incalculable.

While there are hundreds of trade and textbook houses and scores of reprint firms, the test publishers are like reference-book publishers in being few in number. Their names are scarcely known to the book industry, let alone the general public. The largest test publishers are Harcourt, Brace & World; Houghton Mifflin Company; The Psychological Corporation; Science Research Associates; and Educational Testing Services, of Princeton, a nonprofit organization that, interestingly, pays no corporation taxes although it competes explicitly and directly against other publishers who do. Together, the test publishers hardly comprise a large business (during the mid-1960's their net sales as an industry were less than $25,000,000), but their influence on American education is considerable.

Practically every American student is required during twelve years of elementary and secondary schooling to undergo at least two measurements of his relative mental ability, relative in the sense that his test scores are related to his chronological age or to the results obtained from millions of other students in the same year of schooling. Intelligence tests are frequently given during the third and eighth or ninth grades. An even more familiar, and far more prevalent, form of testing is the six or eight measurements of the student's progressive achievements in learning arithmetic, science, English, and other academic disciplines during the years of elementary and secondary education. The American student may also be given tests to determine his individual interests and aptitudes, for purposes of his making salutary judgments about his further education or professional occupation. Actually, in sheer time spent, all of this does not amount to a great deal of testing, no more perhaps than twenty to twenty-five hours during a span of twelve years, even including the "College Boards" that are required of American juniors and seniors who seek enrollment in certain colleges.

It is frequently said of such testing that it inaccurately and unfairly categorizes children, affecting their lives to a degree out of proportion to the meager information that it yields. Yet this kind of testing, which is common to American schools only, does not in fact have so dramatic and possibly irreversible an effect on the lives of students as the examination still administered to some English children at the age of eleven (the famous "eleven-plus"). Given the tendency of Americans to hope that all men are equal in *something*, and given the strong parental pressures on public schools (which are directed neither by the central state, as in France, nor by private bodies, as in the English "public" schools), the rigid classification of students based on formal testing is not so great as some people hold. Indeed, it seems not to have occurred to school officials that if testing is at all desirable, then a possible answer to those who criticize it as an inadequate measure of student abilities and interests is to administer *more* tests rather than fewer. Were intelligence tests, for example, given *each* year from grades three through eight, not only would there be less danger that a student is judged on the basis of his performance during a single hour when he possibly feels intimidated by an unfamiliar procedure or is by chance not feeling well, but also we would come closer to using such tests effectually as a measure of the progressive accretion of knowledge and learning skills through schooling.

Even if one sensibly recognizes that the effort of mass education, as in America, demands the use of measurements other than the individual judgments of teachers, it can hardly be denied that educational tests are in many respects faulty. Some are poorly written, or ambiguously worded; many are outdated. I find it ironic, however, that the scholarly critics of educational testing have not recognized that in large measure its improvement must depend, finally, on a better understanding of the psychology of learning. This discipline has during the past twenty years attracted few scholars and made but little advance. An unfortunate result of this neglect on the part of the universities is to be found in the teaching of reading to children: we are really not clear how people learn to read. But that is another subject, besides being itself the universal American parlor game, a game in which anyone can play if he has a hazy memory of his own childhood and a modicum of anxiety about his children.

Once, one of my colleagues wrote George Bernard Shaw asking for permission to reprint *Arms and the Man* and, on being refused, he wrote again to suggest that an American publisher could, if he wished, print the play without permission, for by then the legal limit of copyright had run out (in the United States the limit is fifty-six years following publication of a work, whereas in Britain it is fifty years following the author's death). Shaw was now piqued into relating, by way of reply, the story of Count Leo Tolstoy, who, in the last years of his life at Yasnaya Polyana when he sought to put away worldly things and lead the simple life, gave away the copyrights of his works and allowed them to be published free of royalties. The sale of Tolstoy's works fell immediately, said Shaw, drawing the lesson that the public does not value what is given away. There is always, of course, the question of what creates value, and the subsidiary question of whether what holds true of commerce is at all relevant to literature. It is the first principle of both that scarcity has the effect of making things dear. Some medieval manuscripts are cherished though they are hardly worth reading; and it has been noted that wartime shortages can make the most unworthy books salable. A truer source of value is that kind of rarity that does not depend on there being but a few copies of a book in existence. A book that is created from a writer's passion, from his search for reality, is a rare thing and ought to be valuable because it is uncommon and unrepeatable. This is the measure, I think, that the publisher does well to use in judging belles-lettres, just as he must take up the measure of utility, which is another kind of value, in judging works whose literal purpose is to inform and educate. In books, value is hard to come by, and hard to lose. The serious reader, no less than the serious writer and publisher, should be concerned not with indulgences but with good works.

A Rage to Learn

Catch phrases do not carry one far. If, as George Meredith said, a proverb is but a halfway house to an idea, then something of the order of "this is one world" can hardly be more than a quarter-house. Formulating axioms about our inhabiting one world is a literary exercise that is at once effortless and grandiose and can be compared to Faulkner's Nobel Prize statement that "man will not merely endure, he will prevail," which poses a hardly meaningful distinction, or C. P. Snow's "we die alone," which offends F. R. Leavis and the precise grammarian. The world is not less nor more than what it has been, a whole of many parts. Even today the astronaut lands in a particular place when he comes home.

The dynamics of worldwide transport and communication, which understandably give rise to our hopes for universality, are not strictly modern or even progressive. In the ninth century the trade and general concourse between Arab and Latin was fluid and frequent, yet today an Italian cannot travel from Israel into the Lebanon but must first be neutralized in a place like Crete. Erasmus wrote to scholars across the continent and their dialogues proceeded on common assumptions. The East was mysterious to them, and inaccessible, but then again, today there is not a single known observer from the United States to be found in China. The world's peoples, as such simplified illustrations may remind us, have a stubborn way of drawing together only to pull apart again. Even the exchange of literature—surely the most international of goods—is always discounted by the particularities of language, of nationality, and of politics.

Language is a powerful instrument of divisiveness, and even the same language can separate a people, as Shaw said of the Irish and the English. The British publisher, for example, sells about half of his books outside the United Kingdom but only a token amount to the largest English-speaking country in the world, the United States. He cannot in most instances sell directly to the Americans because of contractual restrictions; rather, he exchanges licenses or rights with American publishers. Before World War II the rate of exchange was heavily in favor of the British—more English books were published in the United States than American books in Britain—but it has since then been reversed and today the British publisher is twice the buyer that he is the seller. Yet the exchange rate in exporting and importing literary rights makes no great difference in dollars or pounds sterling. Jonathan Cape made more money from obtaining English rights to Ernest Hemingway's books than he did, most likely, from the sales of a dozen English authors of indifferent talent. Even without distinct financial advantage as a lure, both British and American publishers have at times been tempted to set up shop across the sea. Macmillan and Oxford still maintain relatively small American branches but others, including Cape and Heinemann and Longman, did not persist in New York. The general lack of success of such ventures has confirmed the tendency of publishers to sell books directly only to their nationally defined areas. Hence, the London publisher still sells as freely to Australia as before, but his market in Israel has declined since 1947. Trade may follow the book, as Sir Stanley Unwin pronounced years ago, but it is also true that in the past the book has most profitably followed the flag. It is perhaps not surprising that the Americans have not, until recently, sold a large number of books outside their own country, and proof that they are bumbling imperialists might be found in the fact that their sole former colony, the Philippines, and their largest present dependency, Taiwan, are notorious pirates of American copyrights.

Given their patterns—and their limitations—neither British nor American book publishing has in its international form changed much over the past half-century, but now, as the Common Market looms higher and threatens to create unfavorable balances of trade for them, they will both need to find new ways with vigor and imagination. The comfy, cottage aspect of British publishing that the English themselves seem to find so reassuring has always been, I think, largely pretentious, and it is certainly an anachronism in these times. There is, too, a certain smugness in the American publisher who, looking abroad myopically, sees the opportunities of cheap labor in buying printing and engraving but ignores the fact that this very labor is growing into an audience of readers. On both sides of the Atlantic, book publishing should be re-examined in the light of the altered state of the English language itself, the weakened distinction between the use of so-called general books and educational books, and the demand for reading material by the "emerging" peoples of Africa, South America, and Asia.

As English becomes the first language around the world its Anglo-American proprietorship will be somewhat diluted. Books are nowadays being published *in English* in The Netherlands and Japan as well as in India and Ghana. Thus far these are chiefly scientific and reference works, but within another decade "foreign" publishing in English may broaden in scope, and the British and Americans may discover that they no longer own the language. (One cannot but shudder to think what the

Japanese will do with the noblest of modern tongues, especially if they mistake gracefulness for politeness.) This phenomenon is not the result entirely of the fact that cheaper composition and printing may be obtained in the Far East (or in Europe) than in the English home countries. Rather, it reflects the enormous demand for books in English the world over, a demand so great as even to surmount the extremely high prices of American books, whose exports are increasing at the rate of fifteen per cent a year. Significantly, the largest category of American export is textbooks, and it is to sell textbooks that some New York and Chicago publishers are establishing branches in Tokyo and Mexico City and elsewhere in order to produce books in proximity to new markets at low costs.

The Americans going abroad will enter British markets mainly, and if they *publish* abroad they will soon be able to compete with British books in price. But price is not the primary element in publishing competition: originality of idea and felicity of style are far more important. Different issues face the British and the American publisher. For the former the question is whether he will be flexible and skillful enough to meet the changing needs of his old markets, as in Africa. I cannot believe that the present British textbooks, whose origin is plainly the traditional English system of educating only a part of the populace, will for long attract teachers in other countries (or, for that matter, in Britain itself). These textbooks on almost any level of instruction assume a considerable reading sophistication on the part of the student—not to speak of requiring at least a middle-class home background. What they lack is the stage-by-stage instructive quality that is necessary in teaching peoples who intend to enroll in their schools their *whole* populations. Nor have the British made much use of records, tapes, workbooks, and teachers' manuals as subsidiaries to books. The American, on the other hand, may have to learn to attempt less within the scope of a textbook and not place his audience in the position of the third-grade child who wrote in the usual "book report" that "this book tells me more about penguins than I care to know." The elaborateness of American instructional materials proves to be as tedious for the undereducated as for the advanced learner; its cost is not alone in price but in loss of educational spontaneity.

In Britain the general publishing business has been isolated from technical (or textbook) publishing, and their separation ill serves both. Too often the general publisher is proud to say that he knows nothing about textbooks, but surely this should be regarded as an admission of guilt rather than of taste. No one in the mid-twentieth century can ignore the processes of education and remain contemporary with his time. Calvin Coolidge said in 1925 that the business of his country was business, but today the business of America, as it is in most parts of the world, is education. Education is not only a grand ideal, it is a huge industry. Everywhere there is a rage to learn, as the fastest-selling products of publishing attest, these being textbooks, scientific monographs and journals, reference works, and academic paperback books. If the publisher of general books ignores the temper of our time he risks more than a slight surmise of guilt: his risk may be no less than whether he may continue his patronage and promotion of belles-lettres.

The general publisher (whether he is large or small— the distinction here is not size but *kind* of publishing) probably cannot grow in an expanding economy that tends to inflate prices unless he undertakes to commission and prepare books and related written and spoken materials (including children's books, or "juveniles,") that will sell to large-scale institutional buyers—schools, colleges, libraries. The familiar lament that the small, distinguished publisher—all distinguished publishers are ordained small —cannot survive rising overhead and production costs deplorably misses the point: what he cannot survive is the publishing of too many books of the same order. The output of titles in the United States is obviously excessive, but an output of as many titles in Britain suggests scandalous carelessness when one considers that the British market for books is perhaps a third smaller. For the British especially, a sound way to grow in strength is to broaden the scope of publishing and publish fewer titles at the same time. To do this requires capital but it also requires trained staffs with a sense of urgency born of opportunity. Such people plainly exist in Britain, though they tend to want good pay. It must be admitted that the opportunities in British publishing for young people are poor—and so are the young people. It is still true, presumably, that one would do well to have a private income even as an employee in London publishing. Surely that is a quaint notion in a modern nation.

Such stipulations are, one will recognize, suspiciously American in tone. No doubt the physician prescribes according to his own, rather than the patient's, vision of health. It is hard to escape either your prejudice or your presumption, and as an American who has himself tried to effect a union between his own and British particularities in publishing, and failed, I ought to know this well. Yet the matter of particularity, of representing one part of this one world, is not to be laid aside so easily. The British publisher has discrete resources from which he may draw. However much the language is borrowed by others he continues to be its trustee, and his tradition as a born traveler and visitor is unrivaled, for his books have at one time or another followed the flag to every continent where there was a reader. These are qualities to be admired—and put to use—whether by themselves or in combination with American skills in managing large enterprises and in teaching a large population. Publishers born to the same language *ought* to be able to enlarge the authorship and readership of each other, whatever their tribulations, and, if they are first-rate, they can afford to have short memories and high hopes.

The Tribute of
Practicality

Even allowing for the contrariness of the physical world, and the seeming illogicality of accident, the truth is that we are rarely abused by circumstance. Generally, what happens to a man is like himself. This principle of sorts is worth the attention of publishers, I think, because we tend to excuse ourselves, when things are going rather badly, as being little more than the disinterested medium between the author and the public, with no charge for either. If we can put aside the exhilarating thought (which is a corollary of this grim moralism) that indifferent authors and indifferent audiences *deserve* each other, we may recognize that bad books are in large measure the result of bad publishing and the result, particularly, of the specious assumption that if one publishes more books he will publish more good ones. Of the making of many bad books there ought to be an end.

Yet, having said as much, I confess that the educational publisher of our own time has a compelling reason to be enticed by the promise of reward in issuing more and more books. For there would seem to be no limit to the great contemporary demand for textbooks and other pedagogical works, nor indeed to the proliferation of new learning that must be recorded in books to serve the interest of modernism and progress. This demand for the works of education is not wholly or even distinctively an American phenomenon, of course, but its origins can be clearly comprehended, and perhaps best so, in the context of the social history and the national experience of the United States. Over the course of three centuries Americans have so refined a belief in the practical value and social necessity of educating the *whole* citizenry that this has become our national token. Of the Scots it may be said— with the ease of oversimplification—that they have a passion for facts, which is why they are Presbyterians and engineers; whereas the Jews find delight in abstractions and so excel in philosophy and music. The Russians admire learning when it is both direct and collective and are the world's best lecture audiences. But the Americans seem always to expect of knowledge that it prove itself; from it they must exact the tribute of practicality. It is a concept that influences not only the forms of education in the United States but also the kinds of educational books.

Because, practically speaking, knowledge *can* be made to serve definable, utilitarian purposes, the American educator has tended to divide and subdivide it into "courses of study," with the consequence that the American can almost be generically defined as a taker of courses. One has only to announce the existence of a course, literally on any subject, and some American will enroll in the confidence that he will be given credit for enlightenment! (Who, indeed, but an American could conceive, as has been done, of a course that teaches students how to pass other courses?) Typically, a course of study in secondary schools and colleges is organized with a beginning, a middle, and an end, a schema that is not so elementary as it seems. European universities are not nearly so dependent as the American upon systematics in teaching (not scholarship, but teaching), nor upon the division of teaching into measured units of time. The European lecturer moves from topic to topic at his own pace, and he is not usually under a compulsion to make his observations fit within a corpus. Perhaps more significant in American teaching than a limited definition of subject matter is its rigorous sense of time: classroom sessions uniformly encompass fifty minutes, are convened three or five times a week over a period of twelve or eighteen weeks, and all together these units are computed to equal "credits" of instruction. (So far as I know, no one has investigated the psychological effects on teaching of such precise schedules—or related them to an obvious analogue, those restrictions put upon dramatists and performers in American commercial television, which is organized into programs of twenty-nine or fifty-nine minutes divided into three or four equal parts.) The tendency to systematize is pervasive. Even in the more amorphous fields of study, such as sociology, an instructor tends to give to his subject a categorical form, hence the practice of listing in college catalogs, under the titles of courses, rubrics like "backgrounds—principles—problems" and "theory—applications."

The conception of teaching per courses underlies in good part the use of textbooks. With a textbook at hand, both the teacher and the student are better able to know where they have been and where they are going. Textbooks, in short, not only point the way but also keep a record of the progress. Now this statement will offend the sensibilities of that liberal, progressive teacher who deplores any kind of *prescription* in teaching (and who may unconsciously oppose the use of textbooks in part because of their very name—"text" having, as it does, echoes of scripture and authority). Yet there is, in the peculiar nature of American education, a pragmatic need for both course-teaching and textbooks of one kind or another. We are the first, and perhaps still the only, people who have attempted to educate an entire population. We perforce use such styles and systems of teaching as will accommodate millions upon millions of learners of incredibly diverse experience and competence. American education has, I think, accomplished its aim without yielding too radically to the dangers of conducting a mass exercise. A textbook is in one sense an antidote to such dangers: at the very least it enforces the *privacy* of reading.

The exigencies of trying to teach literally everyone in a society have led, not surprisingly, to experimentation with means of instruction quite different from books. The textbook publisher has no hegemony. As secondary school and college enrollments increase at a rate faster than the nation's population as a whole, it becomes fashionable to predict that television teaching, the use of filmstrips and other projectional devices, and even teaching machines will substantially replace the traditional textbook. While the publisher can confute such predictions, I think, he can hardly ignore their implications; nor can he assume that books are confirmed in their acceptance. It is easier to become a reactionary than a liberal, if harder to persist as one. Some years ago I heard a publisher calm the fears of printing unions by insisting that manuscripts will always be composed by hand, that type will continue to be plated, and that paper will forever be moved across plates in order to be printed. Leonard Shatzkin, who was formerly the production chief of Doubleday, said at that time that he felt as if he were attending a convention of harness-makers in the year 1903. (Mr. Shatzkin's ingenuity is not confined to wit. I have yet to tell him that one Doubleday book I bought, *The Sleeping Partner,* employed the most interesting use of paper since the appearance of Henry Miller's *Air-Conditioned Nightmare:* each thirty-two-page form differed in color and in weight. This is, no doubt, a way to clear out one's inventory in the name of Art.)

It cannot make a publisher a reactionary, confronted though he is by the brave new world of universal and experimental education, to state that the advantage that books hold over other means of instruction is precisely the discreteness of reading. Reading is a private act, like reflection. Television and motion pictures and recordings are all public means of obtaining information, and their shortcomings as instructional instruments should be obvious when one considers that learning can only in a limited sense become a group activity. (Students are usually tested in groups but never *as* a group.) In reading, as in the best teaching, there is a simple equation between two persons: opposite the reader is the writer, who has had also to engage in a private act. Writing is inherently individual in a way that no public means of imparting information can be. (Not too much should be claimed for textbooks in this respect, compared with other kinds of writing. Reading *The Education of Henry Adams* is a more subtle and rewarding act of reflection than reading any textbook I know of.) To protect the place of books in the processes of education the publisher is better served, finally, by improving the style and refining the substance of his publications rather than by emulating, however that might be possible, those other means of instruction that are contrary to books in purpose and in kind. This is a plain prescription for success, is it not? Yet no publisher will be deceived that it is as easily followed today as in the rather undistinguished past, when educational publishing was a relatively simple business in the United States, because education was simpler, too.

On the 26th of February, 1810, the Reverend Mason Locke Weems wrote to his employer, a publisher, from Augusta, Georgia. He was the same Parson Weems who wrote the biography of the Father of Our Country, but his letter has a ring of truth that is lacking in his book *The Life and Memorable Actions of George Washington*, in which appears the edifying and immortal story of the cherry tree.

"I have at length commenc'd the business to which you have so long press'd," wrote the Parson to his employer, "and for which my friends are pleas'd to say I am peculiarly qualified, to push off books at Court houses and amoung throngs of Country People. I have tried it now but at 2 Courts, Washington & Sparta: and under great disadvantages, for of the 10,000 books that are published & constantly ask'd for I certainly have not more than one hundred varieties & of these many so costly & ponderous as to preclude all hope of sale, or slow at best. . . . Now if from so very imperfect a Collection, a collection in which there is not a single Bible of any sort, nor a Dictionary, nor a Latin book, nor Greek book, nor French book, nor Dream book, nor Horse Doctor's—I say if from so very imperfect a collection I sold in two weeks 6 to 600 Doll what might I not do with a full collection. . . . But Behold! instead of making up handsome little saleable assortments, the very first thing you did was to crush my Heart & Soul by sending 10,000 Dolls worth of your heavy Books, such as had been tried, *most ruinously for me,* in former disastrous times. I may have been a week or two longer in unpacking, & assorting, & packing again those books, but the bitterness of the season . . . Wet, cold, feverish, thirsty, hungry, bad roads, wintry weather, floods, Robbers, fatigue, unprofitable labours, wasting life, an indigent family, all these evils and many others, which I had daily to encounter, were not bad enough, and heavy enough to crush me down, but you must in every letter be imploring of God to send His 'maledictions' and 'curses' after me. . . . And yet, after all I feel no hate, nor wish to do you any harm, but on the contrary, wish most heartily to do you & your family the greatest possible good. . . . In my letter, tomorrow by way of Charleston, I shall point out to you the path to wealth. In the interim, send me off instantly 2 to 300 Doll worth of the best school books."

Little more is known of Parson Weems's publishing career, but he died happy, full of years and presumably remembered by the friends he made at Court houses and among throngs of Country People. Of his employer I know nothing, but can surmise that he came to a bad end, selling shares in his firm to the public and spending his last days surrounded by accountants, management consultants, and public-relations men who, alas, did not even appease his vanity by thinking him a ruthless businessman but, instead, bookish and naïve.

What Parson Weems was selling, in the early nineteenth century, was a list of general books. Without the professional necessity to relate one book to another in any kind of curricular scheme, he offered these to schoolmasters and to the few existing boards of education—his "Court houses," so named because the boards were elected bodies (as they are now). Publishers did not base their business on textbooks per se for the reason that there were few defined courses of study to which books could be matched; indeed, there was small agreement on what should be taught, owing to the absence of compulsory, universal education. Given methods of study that varied widely from village to village, let alone from state to state, the early American publisher depended upon an eclectic (and somewhat eccentric) list to satisfy the still-scant demands of the schools. An enterprising publisher— as Weems complained his employer was not—would offer Latin and Greek grammars, a Bible, histories of England and of the United States, a dictionary, and (after Noah

Webster) a speller. Beyond the elementary drill in reading, spelling, and arithmetic, a schoolmaster followed his
own dictates and was not bound by the requirements of
higher education, whether of secondary school or college.
It was possible for a boy, at least until mid-century, to
pass from grammar school to college with only a bit of
reading or tutoring on the side. Under these conditions,
textbook publishing did not develop into a separate business until the latter part of the century, when the states
established public schools under general-education bills.
It was, in its early days, to take on an unsavory aspect.
Because of the chance for peculation furnished by some
state legislatures, a number of publishers conspired to
form a trust. Beatrice Webb, touring America at the turn
of the century, came upon "the organiser of the Book
Trust," who was, she wrote in her diary, "a thorough-
going American who believed in rotation of office and in
the spoils system. . . . The Book Trust supplied five-
eighths of the school books in the United States, spent
three-quarters of a million dollars annually on agents and
their expenses. They are known to bribe school committees and teachers. . . ." Mrs. Webb, as a Fabian, was
probably less disheartened by villains of this sort than by
the rustic small-town Americans who lounged in the hotel
lobbies, barbershops, and saloons "checked by indecision
as to where to go," who were, she wrote, "not promising
material for a reform movement." Everyone, seemingly,

has wanted to improve the Americans, and none more avidly than the American himself.

As for most aspects of American society, the great watershed of change in education occurred at the turn of the century. The rise of industrialism gave rise to the cities—and to the opportunity for people to rise *in* the cities. America was making good its promise: its society was again the *tabula rasa,* the clean slate on which everyone could begin anew, given only the chance to learn. As education came to be regarded as a social necessity—and, because of the immigrants, a political one—it assumed national rather than local characteristics. Primary and secondary education throughout the United States became more uniform, more predictable. A standard curriculum, based on a graded progression of "skills" that the student was expected to master, was adopted from state to state. The teaching of teachers became, at least quantitatively, the chief concern of colleges. By 1914 it was possible to assume that a course in American history would be taught in either the seventh or eighth grade not only in New York but in Alabama and California. What is more, it could be assumed that the students in that course, across the nation, were using the same kind of textbook. The schools inscribed a pattern, the publishers issued books to fit it, and in that gradual transmutation that became usual over the past half-century, the books made the course as often as the course made the books.

This sea change in American education arose from a number of sources, the most determinant of which was mass immigration into the United States. Tens of millions of immigrants poured in, Germans and Scandinavians toward the end of the century, Slavs and Italians somewhat later, until 1921, when the gates were lowered. For the schools, immigration of such magnitude made their urgent and singular job that of teaching English and citizenship. To accomplish it they fell back on a relatively simple uniform curriculum for all students; and, for a time, they put aside any impulse to give separate training to groups of students who could be segregated according to their varying abilities. (Such segregation would not, in any event, have suited the aim of making American citizens, all of whom were deserving of the same start in the pursuit of happiness.) It was factories that brought the immigrants; it was the immigrants who swelled the towns into cities; and it was the rise of cities that enforced the creation of school *systems,* rather than mere schools. There was, moreover, the phenomenon of America's constantly traveling population—Mrs. Webb mistook the aimless crowds in hotel lobbies for loungers when in fact they were transients—and this restlessness, which has scarcely diminished over a half-century and still amazes the rest of the world, had a singular effect on both teaching and educational publishing. A fifth-grade child from Pennsylvania was likely to appear in the sixth grade in Illinois, and he deserved to be accommodated by a certain consistency in the curriculum and in the books it prescribed.

All of these changes encouraged the growth of textbook publishing, which during the past thirty or forty years found its opportunity in a steadily increasing market of definable dimension. For the first time in American publishing a single book could sell millions of copies in a free market (the textbook trust was a thing of the past, broken under the Sherman and Clayton acts, though politicking of a less-obvious and less-organized sort has never been wholly abandoned by some publishers). A salesman could now carry a small, manageable list and, what is more, he could sell it conveniently to entire school *systems*, not just single schools. No longer, as is still partly the custom in Canada, were publishers compelled to produce books according to local specifications and, frequently, ones written by local authors. Now they could afford to commit large sums of money and careful editorial preparation toward the publication of a basic textbook or series of textbooks. The economics of textbook publishing became integral to the practices of American education: basic lists and concentrated selling resulted in a rapid turnover of books and in ample profits, which in turn enabled publishers to offer the schools not only planned instructional programs but also a variety of practical teaching aids. Educators responded to the assistance of publishers by becoming increasingly contingent upon them, and their collaboration remained fairly uncomplicated until the day the Russians ventured into space.

It demonstrates the deep consciousness of education in the United States, its force as the national *Geist,* that so many Americans immediately saw in Sputnik a challenge not to their military but to their schools. That the Russians, who, like the Americans, believe in universal compulsory education with a pragmatic philosophy, could achieve primacy in space exploration suggested that they had adapted their training systems to produce specialists of a high order, if not, indeed, an entire elite of scientists and technicians. It also suggested that the United States must recast its patriotic slogan from "Make Americans" to "Make Americans more excellent faster." The American Legion has never been quite the same since. What happened, in broader terms, is plain enough. We are suddenly aware that this is no longer a raw industrial society requiring large numbers of semiskilled and unskilled laborers to produce basic capital goods. It is transforming into a refined and extremely specialized industrial complex that demands highly skilled and versatile workers. To manipulate the machinery of the space age—and even to consume its products—requires more sophisticated manipulators.

Schools and colleges are being urged now to diversify and intensify their curriculums, to provide special training for students according to their abilities and interests, to separate the bright from the dull and possibly liberate both. For example, there have developed in recent years not only three or four courses in general (introductory) science for junior high school students, whereas there was previously only one, but also a number of varying approaches to the basic concepts of science. The schools are attempting to introduce a greater range of subjects at all grade levels. This is not being done, as in the spirit of "progressive education" in the 1930's, to give the child more freedom but, rather, to give him more work. There is, in consequence, an inevitable competition for the student's time. It should be obvious—though apparently it is not—that an elementary school child cannot be expected to undertake full courses in reading, mathematics (Sputnik did away with arithmetic), spelling, science, social studies, foreign languages, music and art, and physical education *during the same day*. Certain disciplines will inevitably prevail, likely those that most directly meet the new requirements of our society. In the near run, at least, the schools are likely to follow two current trends in American political policy: first, our dependence for economic and military prowess on scientific and technological skills; second, our dependence for peace on international alliances. Accordingly, the most insistent demands today are for the acceleration of study in mathematics, science, and foreign languages—and to these will soon be added an amalgam of social and behavioral sciences. Teaching English and citizenship is still the job of the schools (and urgently so in those places where the new immigrants, the Puerto Ricans, Cubans, and Mexicans, are clustered), but it is no longer the consuming aim of American education.

It will hardly surprise the contemporary publisher that the conventional textbooks are being questioned as suitable teaching apparatus at a time when so many new things are happening. Nor should he wonder that his old-time collaboration with the schools and colleges has been disturbed by the fact of *their* changing. He now has, in effect, to cancel the old contract and renegotiate his interest—like the Emperor Francis Joseph, who declared his Concordat with Rome at an end in 1870, the year the Pope became Infallible, on the grounds that one of the contracting parties had changed. He has, for one thing, to contend with the government. The process of nationalization, which sixty years ago was confined to a voluntary standardization of the curriculum by the schools, has now taken a new turn: the federal government is increasingly supporting and influencing education with its massive funds, and it has entered the textbook business. Within the span of five years several publicly financed academic groups have coalesced to create educational materials in the fields of physics, chemistry, biology, geology, foreign languages, and English. For the most part, the government is demanding of the schools and colleges that they accelerate and, at the same time, deepen their presentation of basic subject matter. In this respect it has been able, through its commissions and study groups, to lead teachers with more authority than any publisher has ever presumed. (Interestingly, some of the government-produced textbook materials are about as prescriptive as the commercial ones, despite the common protestations of college instructors that traditional textbooks leave too little to the teacher's discretion.)

One way or another, the schools will get what they need to make education relevant and practical to our time. During the first excitement following Sputnik, and under the stringent criticism of university professors who seemingly had just discovered the existence of lower education, it appeared that what was *not* needed was the customary "complete" textbooks, books that attempted to encompass the entire subject matter of a course with lengthy, comprehensive texts and profuse illustrations. This is not so certain now, for even the government-sponsored textbooks tend to be of this kind, however difficult and advanced is their subject matter and however many "supplementary" materials they recommend. What does appear likely is that educational books will be broadened in definition to include not only basic textbooks but also a number of classroom-oriented books smaller in size and more specialized in treatment. There is, too, the evidence of a trend toward what is called by publishers and teachers, with an invidious discrimination, "enrichment" reading, especially in the form of paperback books. Paradoxically, the present-day publisher is well on the way toward imitating his nineteenth-century predecessors by issuing larger and larger lists to accommodate a more relaxed, more diffuse curriculum. It is likely, as well, that the publisher will need to create, even more extensively than in the past, elaborately articulated programs of instruction in which numerous elements—tapes, records, films, laboratory devices—are orbited about the nucleus of a basic textbook. In mathematics, as one instance, this might entail the furnishing of certain manipulative devices (like the Cuisenaire rods) for small children and, for the older ones, slide rules, abacuses, and computers.

All such opportunities will summon a venturesomeness of spirit, not to speak of a great deal of money. They ought, as well, to call for a *rapprochement* between those old partners in education, the teacher and the publisher. Textbook publishing is always fair game for the layman who would find faults in American schooling, but it is not a great sport because it is too easy. School boards and disappointed parents, no less than frustrated patriots and religious bigots, find it complicated and wearying to complain of the nature of school buildings and teaching staffs, but they can readily decry textbooks, which are not only alien, being produced outside the local community, but also convenient to criticism, being both quotable and portable. It taxes the spirit to find so many educators and critics discovering in educational publishing the *deus ex machina* that prevents more sophisticated and advanced materials from being taught in the schools.

This may seem a peevish generalization, yet it readily can be supported. There is a recent specific instance of criticism of educational publishing that lacks both originality of idea and a dependable source of scholarship. A volume of more than five hundred pages, by James J. Lynch and Bertrand Evans, *High School English Textbooks* (Little, Brown, 1963), attempts to evaluate the most widely used books in the public schools. Among its recommendations to editors of literature anthologies are these: that they should include great literature and shun "nonliterature"; that they eschew the abridgment or rewriting of selections in anthologies; that they reduce the editorial apparatus in the books and make what remains more sophisticated and more relevant to teaching criticism of literature (as opposed to teaching social values); that they concentrate on literature of the past; that they cease fearing that students will find great literature "too difficult." For grammar and composition books Lynch and Evans recommend that these be so constructed as to avoid the repetition of subject matter from year to year, that they treat literature as the central subject for student writing instead of "home, friends, school, and community," and, finally, that the books should not be inhibited by the presumptions held by some authors that learning grammar is a difficult task or that a subject can be made easier when lengthy attention is devoted to it. The authors suggest that a single book of about two hundred pages should be used during all four years of high school.

For the most part one can readily agree to such pre-scriptions. When it comes to sin, as Calvin Coolidge reported the pastor to say, we are all against it. I confess to believing that first-rate literature is better than second-rate literature, and I affirm that if someone can learn some-thing the first time around, there is no point in teaching it to him a second time. The trouble with such affirmations, quite apart from their ingenuousness, is that they do not assist the high school English teacher in solving some of her most serious problems—problems arising from the deficiencies in her students' earlier training (and home backgrounds), from inadequate facilities, from the incom-plete grouping of students of different abilities, etc., etc. Professors Lynch and Evans ignore most such problems. They *could* maintain, I suppose, that these are outside the scope of their book, but, of course, a publisher who offers a literature program to the schools is not allowed such a plea.

High School English Textbooks proceeds on several stated or implicit assumptions: (1) There is no problem of censorship in textbooks; one need not worry about print-ing good literature that mentions sex or that uses words presumably offensive to racial and religious groups.

(2) There is no cause to "cater" to students who do not read proficiently and do not care about the critical values of literature, and who happen to abound in great numbers in the schools. (3) Teachers generally have the skill, and the time, to prepare a course of study in literature; all they need is the reading matter. (4) Educational psychology is not germane to teaching literature. (5) Book editors are never denied permission to reprint copyrighted works. (6) There is reason to believe that students, or quite a few of them maybe, possess a high degree of intelligence, a common cultural background, mature experience, as well as abundant self-motivation. Elsewhere than in this book, Professor Evans has spoken (with the coy use of a neologism) of "educationalicists," and, given his assumptions, one perceives how he has indeed kept himself free of the earthier problems that face these scorned professionals, such problems as exist in Chicago, New York City, Philadelphia, Los Angeles, Miami, and elsewhere. He is apparently fond of repeating that literature is the proper subject of English, but this statement does not go far enough: one must ask, as well, what literature is about, whom it concerns, and why it is required to be taught to everyone.

However limited Lynch and Evans may be in their approach to literature anthologies, their statement on grammar and composition books is not merely limited but is a shocking instance of college teachers of English who plainly do not know enough about the development and uses of the several English grammars. Their position is that no grammar should be taught in the high school that is not immediately applicable to the problems of composition. Despite their oracular statements about literature being the proper subject of English, they explicitly deny that grammar is itself a proper subject of English teaching. Professor Evans apparently does not take grammar seriously, and this leads him to propose that a hundred pages of it are better than a thousand pages. Moreover, Lynch and Evans seem to be unconcerned with what has happened in the research and teaching of linguistics during our time—there is no significant mention of this in their book.

Reading this book I was reminded that Professor James Sledd wrote in *The English Journal* of May 1960 an educated attack on Bertrand Evans's position on teaching grammar (as it was stated in *The Educational Forum* of January 1959). This exchange ought to be read by those many English teachers who are worried about rumors of an argument—whose terms are falsely posited—between "traditional" and "linguistic" grammars. Professor Sledd concludes, among other things, that Professor Evans's "concept of descriptive grammar must be pathetically limited. I suppose he hopes and thinks that most teachers know and teach some traditional handbook of grammar and that such a handbook treats 'the forms and functions' of all the important grammatical elements in English. . . . The biggest of all the questions which Evans begs is just the question of which grammar shall be taught. . . ." Evans begs it, again, in *High School English Textbooks*, by simply suggesting that less is more, an axiom that presumably can be applied to any old grammar.

If grammar is not worth a formal and concerted study in the schools, then the teaching of accurate, graceful writing is, according to this book. Just how such writing *can* be taught, and, further, whether indeed it can be taught in any pragmatic relation to the study of grammar are questions the authors prefer to ignore. Yet they are quite firm in their belief that writing in the high school ought to have as its subject matter those works of literature the student is concurrently reading. One wonders if they have seen many examples of high school student writing on "literary" subjects. One wonders, too, what the course of literature over the centuries would have been had writers been warned against writing about themselves.

Education is too serious a business to suffer largely irrelevant criticism and, like it, publishing deserves, on the field, the courtesy of more informed adversaries. That there is much amiss in the teaching of English, and in the textbooks that are employed by teachers, is obvious. It is also obvious that a sensible way to determine what can be a more disciplined and skillful teaching of English is to begin with the schools and with society as both are today. The present, as Warren G. Harding might have said, always comes before the future.

Probably, good textbooks ought not to need justifying. Bad textbooks ought not to be bought. Publishers seem always, self-consciously, to speak of the important service they render the schools and colleges and, in turn, the grave responsibility they owe to these institutions. These are not unworthy sentiments, but they cause embarrassment precisely because they may be applied to any product and any customer, not only to books but to meat packing. The best service a publisher can render to the schools is to sell them good textbooks; the best service they, as customers, can render the publisher is not to buy ill-written, poorly edited, and cheaply manufactured books. It is possible to be this tough-minded in the book-publishing industry, I think, because it is one of the strong-holds of capitalistic competition. What is competition in this sense? It occurs when entrepreneurs speak always to their customers and rarely to each other.

Textbooks are not works of literature and seldom do they display original, mint scholarship—one always searches for examples after bravely citing William James's *Principles of Psychology,* but with small success. Yet one need not revive the old and trite antagonism between belles-lettres and educational writing by confusing their separate functions. I once tried to dispel this confusion in an exchange of views with the Carnegie Foundation. (To draw on Samuel Johnson's remark about scoundrels, the last refuge of a man defending a vested interest is, if not patriotism, to quote his own arguments.) The *Bulletin* of the Foundation described an experimental course at Brown University and quoted its president as saying that "most textbooks are hardly worth reading; if not barren of ideas, they are impoverished in that respect." That text-books are not the end of college study hardly needs to be advanced, nor should it be necessary to explain that, in providing a systematic introduction to a field of study, textbooks are a means of saving time—time that a teacher can spend on his own devices and time that a student can spend on more subtle, varied reading. It is futile to com-plain of textbooks, given the persistence of course-teaching in the schools and colleges, especially because the wise teacher will use a textbook at his own pace and in his own way. "One does not blame the adze," I wrote, "if the shipwright is lazy or incompetent or merely tired, unless, of course, the shipwright fashioned his own adze, which is what teachers do when they write textbooks."

It will not do, as I must be reminded, to be vexed because the world refuses to wait on old privileges, even if it is consoling to reflect that the world waits on old books, which always have something important to say to new people. Still, consolation is the temporary surcease of feeling rather than the resolution of its cause. There *is* a searching for excellence in education, and teachers *are* tacking this way and that in order to fulfill changing necessities. In our milieu there is a strong inflation in learning, and more and more books are needed as currency. It is safe, too, if the metaphor can stand the weight, to assume that there is a kind of contrary Gresham's law at work, so that good books drive out bad books. The place of the book in education may be simply demonstrated. One teacher, given time and independence, can shape a program of learning. Two teachers can do the same but they will, in addition, seek a common reference. The book is the common reference, and the reason, finally, for the presence of many books is that, while learning is enduring, it is never fixed.

The Editorial
We

Soon or late, one must ask the question of a book: Is it really good? The critic asks the question after its publication, the publisher before. (Publishers have been known to wait on publication: the legend persists that the chairman of one of America's largest houses once said that "a good book is a book that sells good.") It is a simple question but so germane, so plainly the gist of criticism, that it can be asked even of civilizations. I recall once when it was. During a party given for some members of the United Nations I found myself besieged by an obstreperous Indian, not Krishna Menon but someone with his usual bad manners. "You Americans," he said, "are the world's adolescents and, like a street gang, a danger to older people. Of course you are only three hundred years old, which is very young compared to our own civilization of three thousand years." A Chinese, who had been standing quietly by, then politely asked: "But it wasn't really a first-rate civilization, was it?"

The question of whether books are first-rate needs to be asked not only for its relevance to authors but also to editors. Editors in publishing houses are increasingly involved in the actual writing of books; they have given a pungent meaning to the old journalistic phrase "the editorial we," which stands for a common opinion that is written by a single person. Whether an editor *ought* to be as important as he now seems to be in the making of books is still another question, but we may be content to regard him as a necessary middleman, who in commerce is a man who makes goods move by standing in the way.

It is well known that the editing of textbooks is a far more intensive and (I suppose) demanding pursuit than the editing of fiction and nonfiction. The textbook editor, more often than the general-book editor, is likely to seek out an author and suggest to him not only a particular subject but also the form and direction of his writing. Accordingly, the editor feels entitled to assume a central role in the eventual creation of the work. Given this privilege, he should also be expected to maintain a standard of discriminating taste in editing. As in all criticism, it is easier to say what this is not, rather than what it is. Presumably everyone will agree that if a nice judgment is to be exercised in textbook editing, then it will not tolerate bad writing, yet the fact is that educational editors allow to be printed a grotesque amount of syntactically careless, inaccurate, and inflated language.

73

Elementary textbooks, it seems to me, have improved steadily over the years in almost all respects except style, and while their subject matter is admirably up-to-date, so, regrettably, is their jargon. High school textbooks are somewhat better written, and college books still better (excepting those textbooks for courses in educational methods and, possibly, sociology). This ascending scale suggests that as the editor desists the writing improves, for it is commonly true in publishing that the editor is most directly engaged in a book at the elementary school level and least so at the college level. An irate college textbook author once sent me a statement from a European, whose identity I do not know, that condemns the "authorship" of editors: "My own experiences in this field have been so crushing that I cannot think of any other country in which they could have happened. If I send a manuscript to America, I must anticipate that it will not be respected as the inalienably personal expression of a man who thinks and writes in this fashion, and in no other. It will be treated on the superstitious notion that an opera, if it is written by ten composers, will be ten times better than if written by one."

This is a fair indictment, I think, especially as so many textbook editors believe that they command writing skills at least as great as that of their authors, a belief supported by the generally poor performance of secondary teachers and college instructors as writers. Higher education in the United States, for whatever reasons, does not reliably produce in its graduates an *expertise* in fluent and clear writing. Admittedly, there are no simple solutions to this problem, and one may reasonably wonder whether good writing can be taught at all. (A popular thesis of those critics who say that grammar is presently taught in an inadequate way is that thorough training in descriptive grammar would also improve the writing skills of students, but so far as I know, there is no evidence that this is true.) Yet it can be deduced that college instructors, if one is to judge by their own writing, do not demand much of their students and so tend to perpetuate a barely serviceable, if hardly pleasing, standard of educated expression.

If the universities are negligent in this respect, then so are the publishers. Editors are probably undone by embracing a double standard: they expect more of themselves than of their authors, whose writing might improve were editors less tolerant and were they to refuse to "fix" manuscripts that lack clear, spare, and engaging expression. A fallacy that all editors commit on occasion is to depend upon the professional qualifications of an author in a particular subject, to the exclusion of the question of whether he writes well. An editor, no less than a critic, must examine precisely what is written, not what is promised. (Even lexicographers ought not to go unchallenged merely because of their profession. The editor of

Merriam-Webster's Third New International Dictionary replied testily to a criticism of still another reference work by saying, "It should be unnecessary to point out wherein this is nonsense unsupported by evidence." Quite apart from the wondrous use of "wherein," we may doubt whether he can be serious. What red-blooded American really wants his nonsense to be supported?) The improvement of authors, if that can be regarded as a responsibility of the publisher, could be better accommodated were it not for the common practice of assigning two or more instructors to write a textbook. Many school and college books are without the impress of style because they are the work of collaboration, oftentimes among teachers who were, until an editor intervened, unknown to one another. It is curious that publishers should continue to believe that committees can write well. None has, save the committee of scholars who in 1611 produced the King James Bible—and even here one suspects, knowing the way of committees, that some poor wretch was left with the work once the prayers were said and Bishop Lancelot Andrewes dismissed the meetings.

There is a reason for the practice of multiauthorship in textbook publishing but it is not, as some editors assume, the necessity to draw on diverse and specialized talents in order to produce a comprehensive work. Rather, the practice persists mainly because publishers have not yet succeeded in persuading the best people in education that the writing of a textbook can be a significant accomplishment, worthy of a full year or two of a man's time. Nor have publishers usually been willing, in support of this contention, to advance monies to an author to the degree that he would be able to write a textbook at times other than weekends and summer holidays, which is when most textbooks are now written. The assignment of duties among a number of authors is, for the most part, an expedient having little to do with the increased specialization of knowledge (after all, a good author can *read* what other scholars have written). On the contrary, it derives from the expectation that each of several authors will give to his textbook writing a lower priority than to his other professional work, not only his teaching but also the preparation of "scholarly" articles and books. In this kind of discrimination the teacher-author is encouraged by the prejudices of university deans and presidents who, in their demands that a professor "publish" in order to be eligible for advancement in salary and in grade, do not count textbooks a creditable form of publishing. It is said to be true—though one could not expect to find explicit proof of it—that in some American universities there is a scale of publishing credit in which eight or ten articles in scholarly journals are "worth" one full-length book, and books are not counted if they are either "popular" or intended as textbooks.

Inattention, like divided attention, will take a toll.

A consequence of creating textbooks by the work of several hands—or of a single hand that is intermittently engaged—is that the publishing process is ludicrously prolonged. Now that publishers are given to explaining the mysteries of their craft to stockbrokers in Wall Street it is quite usual to hear that the preparation of an elementary textbook may require six to eight years, or that a college textbook may be the result of five years' labor. This kind of statement is usually made with a certain pride ("a publisher is not a printer") or as a means of expiating the high cost of large editorial staffs. In this sense pride goes before confusion, for a prime cause of unreasonable delays in textbook publishing is not only multiauthorship but also multieditorship. Editors come and go with maddening frequency. As educational publishing has grown, it has been subject to an occupational hazard that might be called house-hopping, as editors are lured from publisher to publisher by offers of more money and greater prestige. There is no muddle quite like that an author finds himself in when he is confronted by two or three editors sucessively in the course of publishing a single book, especially because each editor will inevitably review and recast what has gone before. This phenomenon is not confined to textbooks. Trade, or general, publishing in the United States has for many years been subject to it. One of the funniest essays by James Thurber (a University of Ohio graduate) describes the arrant enthusiasm of a new editor:

"Dear Jim Thurber: I haven't had the pleasure of meeting you since I had the great good luck to join forces with Charteriss, but I look forward to our meeting with a high heart. Please let me know the next time you are in the city, as I should like to wine and dine you and perhaps discuss the new book that I feel confident you have in you. If you don't want to talk shop, we can discuss the record of our mutual football team. You were at Northwestern some years ahead of my time, I believe, but I want you to know that they still talk about Jimmy Thurber out there. . . . I approve of your decision to resume the use of your middle name. It gives a book dignity and flavor to use all three names. I think it was old Willa Cather who started the new trend, when she dropped the Seibert."

One might surmise that in general publishing, given the fact that manuscripts are usually submitted in complete form and given, also, the presumption that an author (rather than an editor) has chosen a subject and has by himself brought it to fulfillment, there would be little need for the intervention of editors in the actual process of writing. But this is too simple a view of publishing—and of writing. Even the most accomplished writer may demand an intimate attention from his editor. Cyril Connolly, in speaking of Thomas Wolfe and his editor, Maxwell Perkins, found it "unnecessary to point out that American publishers are a dedicated group: they are loyal, generous and infinitely painstaking; they live for their authors and not for social climbing or the books they want to write themselves; they know how to be confessors, solicitors, auditors and witch doctors. . . ." Writing is the loneliest of professions, and the writer, like all artists, tends to exhaust his personal resources: in the dialogue between the writer and the reader there is an uneven exchange, for what enriches the one has depleted the other. (Alberto Moravia, in *Conjugal Love,* symbolizes the fears of a writer that he must preserve himself in order to create; the hero denies himself his wife's bed.) If a writer must borrow assistance, or merely encouragement, then it would seem natural that he turn to an editor who can be expected to be not only sympathetic but also suitably knowledgeable. For the editor this is flattering but dangerous, for he must decide at what point assistance becomes interference.

Sometimes, of course, more is less. The editor finds himself hopelessly lost in the maze of someone else's creation as he suggests this turning and that. This is especially so in the handling of translations of foreign works, which are nowadays being published in the United States and Britain in great numbers. Here the editor must try to understand not alone what the author is saying but also what the translator says the author is saying. On translations it is perhaps best, unless an editor has the competence with languages of a Helen Wolff or a Denver Lindley, to plead *nolo contendere*. But the most excruciating of complications arises when an author writes in his second language, as in the instance of a Korean novelist writing in English about two youthful lovers, whom I shall call here Sook-ja and Chul-foo, who go to a fisherman's shack to engage in their first dalliance. The editor of an American publishing house wrote the author a letter that is, I feel sure, the most remarkable satire (though unintentionally so) on editing that exists:

". . . Because you have been rather vague about all the physical details of the scene, details which I am sure you have visualized in your mind but have not presented to the reader, it ends up by becoming rather ludicrous.

"The scene belongs in the book, and is very important in clarifying the motivation. But it has an entirely uncharacteristic weakness: it is not visual. Throughout the rest of the book you present wonderful visual images which enable the American reader to see your Koreans and their land. Please don't misunderstand me. I am certainly not asking you to write an obscene chapter. Erotic, of course. Obscene, no. I don't know exactly how to make the distinction to you, but several of us here feel that it is more obscene to be vague than to be forthright. After all, this is the first sexual experience for both Sook-ja and Chul-foo, a moment of deep emotion. This has disappeared almost entirely from the scene. What are Sook-ja's feelings? This too must be added, and is perhaps *more important than any-thing else I have to suggest.* The way you handle the scene now, Sook-ja is almost a piece of furniture.

"You should be much more frank in this scene, in a pure and lyrical and idyllic way. After all, these are very young people making love for the first time. By being vague, you simply prepare the ground for a very bad reaction from your readers, since the whole setting is very challenging. No doubt this will be the first time in literature that anyone has made love in a sardine cauldron. And for reasons too complicated to explain in a letter, please call it a *cauldron* throughout, and not a *pot*.

"And this is not all. You further compound the ludicrousness of the scene by confusing two appetites: hunger and sex. It simply will not do to have Sook-ja and Chul-foo eat leftover sardines out of the same cauldron in which they make love. Why shouldn't there be two cauldrons, one for each appetite? Or perhaps they could find some leftover sardines elsewhere in the shack.

"Another point: You have had Chul-foo light a fire under the cauldron a little while before they begin to make love! At that point the reader doesn't think of the idyllic moment, but worries about blisters on Sook-ja's bottom. I'm sorry to be so coarse about this, but these are the reactions you arouse by vague writing. Furthermore, the fact that the shack is in darkness, and that you don't describe the banked fire very clearly, nor the kind of stove

(I believe the Japanese call it a *kama-do*) being used, all adds to the confusion.

"It would be a great mistake to delete this scene, because it adds greatly to the structure of the book. But it must be rewritten entirely, with great care. I think you will have to provide some dim light from the fire in the shack, and give a much clearer visual description. Furthermore, you will have to prepare the reader carefully for the size of the cauldron. Unless you stress its size, the situation will seem impossible. It would help if Chul-foo failed to light a fire under the cauldron, and if it were still kept warm by the ashes underneath. Ashes retain their heat for quite a long time. Then Sook-ja could quite logically climb into the cauldron to keep warm, and Chul-foo eventually, having found sardines elsewhere, could creep in to join her.

"One more detail. What kind of skirt is it that is fastened around Sook-ja's bosom. If Korean skirts do indeed fasten this way, then I think you may lay the groundwork in some detail, explaining just why Chul-foo reached for Sook-ja's bosom to unfasten her skirt. This is part of the general vagueness in physical description.

"I'm afraid a problem exists concerning the word *bottom*. Certainly the cauldron has a bottom, but so has Sook-ja, and no matter how you handle your description of the cauldron, readers will inevitably associate the two bottoms. I am afraid you better do without the word *bot-*

tom entirely, since there are many other words for both kinds of bottom. . . ."

The editing of novels is not usually this complicated, but then, neither is love-making. An occasional absurdity in editing, whatever else it may suggest about his craft, may obscure the editor's finest function, which is in the first instance to *select* manuscripts and authors, rather than to alter either. Publishing succeeds or fails finally on the judgment of which books should be published, and which authors should be encouraged and supported. So important is the editor to both educational and general publishing that neither is conceivable without him.

Indeed, in the small house the publisher and the editor are the same person. Leonard Woolf, in the third volume of his autobiography, *Beginning Again,* gives a remarkable account of the early days of the Hogarth Press, founded by him and his wife, Virginia. The list of books published during the first four years was:

1917   Leonard and Virginia Woolf. *Two Stories*
1918   Katherine Mansfield. *Prelude*
1919   Virginia Woolf. *Kew Gardens*
       T. S. Eliot. *Poems*
       John Middleton Murry. *Critic in Judgment*
1920   E. M. Forster. *Story of the Siren*
       Hope Mirrlees. *Paris*
       Logan Pearsall Smith. *Stories from the Old Testament*
       Gorky. *Reminiscences of Tolstoi*

For this list the total capital expenditure—not including printing and binding costs—was thirty-eight pounds, eight shillings, and three pence, but in keeping his books Leonard Woolf cheerfully notes that he made no charge for overheads, and certainly none for editorial costs, since the publishers were the editors (and on occasion the authors as well). Even in the eighteenth-century beginnings of modern publishing, when the publisher was primarily a bookseller—printing the books at the back of his shop and selling them at the front—his initial step was to choose an author or two, who in turn recommended other authors. In a contemporary instance this is how *Ulysses* was first published by Sylvia Beach, who met James Joyce in her shop, Shakespeare and Company, on the rue de l'Odéon, took his manuscript, published it, and then sold copies from the shop. No publisher was less rewarded financially for an act of courage and faith than Miss Beach, and few authors have been as cavalier and as ungrateful as Joyce, but that is another story.

Only in comparatively recent times, as publishing houses have grown to considerable size, has editing become a separate profession, so that now the editor is identified as being apart from the publisher, and is, indeed, known to authors as an intellectual who is surrounded by businessmen. He is in this way seemingly exalted, but he is likewise deprecated, for if authors believe that an editor has a heart, they may also assume that he is without a purse, and that the real *business* of publishing literature is conducted by his superiors. Authors are rarely consoled by an editor's compassion if it leads to publishing a book that fails. Editors try to please authors and so tend to accept dubious books, but this is not a serious crime against readers, only against authors. It is an unfortunate attitude, and now a common one, that because a publishing house *hires* editors its management perforce consists of financiers whose job is to make money and to prevent editors from losing it. The fact is that in the best publishing houses, whatever their size, there is no clear distinction between editorial judgment and managerial judgment.

Editors have to be tough-minded to survive; actually, they are more accustomed to nay-saying than the most hardened businessman. Manuscripts are easy to get: the trick is not to find manuscripts but to find good ones. A typical trade publisher in New York receives as many as a hundred manuscripts a week, yet he will publish but a hundred books a year; thus the rate of rejection can be as high as fifty to one. A consequence is that editors spend the better part of their days reading and discussing books they will never publish, which makes them skeptical and jaded. (The layman wonders whether all manuscripts are read straight through—and novices will sometimes submit manuscripts with transposed pages in order to find the truth of it. Most manuscripts *are* read in their entirety, though a sensible editor recognizes that one need not eat the whole apple to know it is wormy.) There are no precise measures the editor may use: popular tastes can no more be calibrated than personal affinities. An editor of general books is guided in his choices variously by his personal inclinations, his professional ambitions, his concept of cultural history and its present trends, and intermittent impulses to act positively. Although editors will still explain to an author whose manuscript is rejected that his book is too nearly like others on the current list, the old familiar concept of "balancing" a list is a myth. No one buys a *list* of books, not even booksellers. Finally, whatever one editor rejects for one of these reasons another may accept for the same reason, which accounts for the element of chance that every author finds in publishing, and every investor too.

Editors themselves cannot be held responsible, I am sure, for the condition of a slack tolerance for mediocre books that prevails today, and that makes publishing appear, to those who know better, unseemly cynical. Leonard Woolf, while he did not undertake publishing as his sole business, could still perceive from his own experience that a burdensome overhead tends to cause one to reason somewhat speciously that he can always meet rising expenses by turning out more and more books. The equations in publishing are fairly simple, if rarely learned: a list of one hundred titles does not necessarily produce more profit than a list of fifty; selling ten copies of one book is better than selling five copies each of two books;

and to sell one book at five dollars is better than to sell two at three dollars each, even if all are properly priced. These are equations an editor can trust, but in themselves they cannot form his judgment, which is to be done only by asking the question of a book: Is it really good?—and by answering it with the confidence that the answer makes a difference.

Sex, Crime, and, to a Lesser Extent, Sports

Now and again my colleagues and I are accused of publishing a "dirty book," this being usually a novel in which there are explicit descriptions of the sexual act. In the view of some angry or aggrieved readers, we are guilty of what might be called literary peculation, a new kind of white-collar crime. They assume that the popular success of a particular book is directly owing to the passages in it that describe physical love and, falling headlong through a straight and narrow syllogism, they infer that the publisher and author conspired to include those passages in order to gain sales. When a reader writes to complain, I tend to answer her—for it is invariably a woman—with the rather obvious statement that neither the author nor the publisher invented sex, and that it is undeniable that many serious contemporary writers regard it as an important and legitimate subject for the novel.

Yet, when I say "subject" I am sure I do not use the

right term. It sounds unsophisticated and outmoded. Criticism has so refined our recognition of the subtler elements in the composition of a novel that it seems too simple to talk about a "subject" of writing, just as it does to talk of "plot." (It can be refreshing to recall that E. M. Forster declares the most basic aspect of the novel to be the question of what happens next—"and then, and then . . .") Whether or not it is materially a *subject*, sex is a considerable preoccupation of the contemporary novelist.

One can make a case, of course, that while sex has at all times been of vital interest to writers, only in recent times have they been allowed to be candid about it. Sex has been lurking in the wings of the novel these past two centuries and, though both the writer and the reader have acknowledged in oblique ways each other's awareness of it, it was not generally permitted to show itself. (Music has suffered no such repressions. Someone once said that if Wagner's characters performed on the stage what his music suggests, all the actors would be arrested.) As a separate art form, the novel in English began boldly enough: *Moll Flanders* and *Tom Jones* are fairly open, if also uncomplicated, on the matter of sexual love. But from Defoe and Fielding to the novelists of the late nineteenth century, there has been an attrition of candor about the physical aspects of love. Sex was put out of sight, if not out of mind, in deference to the genteel sensibilities of the reading public. The treatment of sexual love in fiction has been severely subject to the degree that the public (including its police and courts) has been willing to allow realistic expression in published works.

This is not to say that the attitudes held by the reading public at any one time are, in this connection, the sole influence on the writer; nor can the appearance and reappearance of sex in the English and American novel be charted on such a premise. The early nineteenth-century romanticism, for instance, created a vision of ideal love that had the effect of altering the writer's view of sex without any direct relation to the religious and moral codes then prevailing. Moreover, writers who are contemporaries react (or do not react) to the conventions of polite society in quite opposite ways; the same public, presumably, bought the novels of Henry James and Theodore Dreiser, and of John Galsworthy and Frank Norris. We cannot, all in all, assume that the preoccupation with sex by so many novelists is mainly the consequence of more liberal censors.

Indeed, it is probable that today's writers are more seriously convinced that sex is a revelatory, a profoundly meaningful, experience, than are their readers. The writer cannot avoid the demonstrations and proofs that much of contemporary life is dominated by a sameness of experience that follows from the mass production and mass consumption of practically all the things around us. He knows how hard it can be to identify what is personally meaningful. It has been said that sex, crime, and, to a lesser extent, sports are practically the only experiences that are unremittingly individual: each involves a real event in which a human being can be comprehended in an elemental relation to other human beings. It is hardly proof of this proposition, though it may be indicative, that all three activities repeatedly appear in the works of two modern American masters, Hemingway and Faulkner. *The Sun Also Rises* presents an interplay between sex and sport; *To Have and Have Not,* between sex and crime. And it can even be said that in Hemingway's vision, war is a climactic experience that is the combination of sport and crime. Faulkner's concern with sports as a subject includes stunt flying ("Pylon") and hunting; his involvement with sex and crime hardly needs to be illustrated. Beyond their superb handling of technical or naturalistic detail, there is not much critical realism in their treatment of these activities, but this is not to the point here. (Both of them had, in respect to these subjects, the failings of a romantic writer. Hemingway's regard for sports often verges on sentimentality and, in his later works on bullfighting and deep-sea fishing, gives way to it embarrassingly. Faulkner's descriptions of violent sex and crime, read by themselves, are ridiculously antic.)

No one will suggest that a writer must himself resort to crime and sports and, in some special ways, to sex, in order to gain vital, germane experience; or that a writer who has taken a serious or professional part in these is better qualified to write meaningfully than others. Actually, with the possible exception of Sade, and of the former male prostitute and felonist Jean Genet, no criminal other than strictly political offenders has been a writer of note. (Oscar Wilde tried to make a case for the poisoner and essayist Thomas Griffiths Wainewright, but all that is remembered of him now is Wilde's short biography, which repeats the credible story that Wainewright killed his sister-in-law because she had very thick ankles.) Nor has any professional or, at the least, accomplished sportsman (excepting, possibly, flyers) been notably successful as a writer. As for sex, it is an experience that is universal and, by definition, normally ordinary. Probably only Casanova and Sade can claim a place in literature chiefly because of their unique qualifications in the practices of erotic love.

As an experience, sexual love is real, by any definition of reality; it is circumstantial—something *happens* when people are sexually engaged; further, however depersonalizing the sexual act may be, both the anticipation and the recollection of it are, as emotional forces, indicative of personality. The same qualities are apparent in crime and sports. All three are classically the experiences in which human beings believe they can be tested, physically and morally. Because there is in each a conflict, their value as subjects of storytelling, beginning historically with the

Odyssey, is obvious. Yet in contemporary literature, these activities would seem to have a particular essence: they characterize, I think, a recurrent fascination for the brutal life. Sex, crime, and sports are all susceptible to brutality in the sense that each can simply involve the violation of the privacy and, usually, the *person* of a fellow being. The brutal life has, by evidence of literature, a profound significance in the workings of our society. The astonishing spectacle of Jean-Paul Sartre devoting an eight-hundred-page critique to Jean Genet, whose works are almost wholly devoted to the homosexual and criminal underground, suggests that even a metaphysical view can be adduced to it. Both Genet and Sartre have, in this respect, obvious antecedents: the brutal life has been a great twentieth-century subject. It is crucially D. H. Lawrence's subject, and in Lawrence and James Joyce it is revealed by their interest in the simplicities (and, particularly, the supposedly exceptional sexual powers) of the proletarian. Lady Chatterley's gamekeeper is vital because he can be oblivious, and honestly brutal; and his mate could be Joyce's wife (her name was, marvelously, Nora Barnacle), who didn't understand Joyce's writing and shared his hardships but not his doubts. The brutal life is Anderson's subject, and Dreiser's and O'Neill's, more particularly, in their cases, in the form of a hankering for brutalized relationships as a means of unmasking the innermost motivations of middle-class characters. The proofs of this literary obsession are so abundant that one is tempted to protest its exceptions, of which there are of course many, or is inclined to explain it in other terms, such as that we tend to examine the brutal life more attentively because we now know more about it through Freud, and have been made more familiar with it by the literalness and immediacy of picture magazines and television.

It is fairly common for writers and critics to talk about the alienation of the serious writer from society. Some novelists, like Norman Mailer, are so consciously estranged that they are able to write about little else other than this condition. With certain writers it is not a question of their taking a stand against popular opinion, but, rather, standing apart from it. They might be said to suffer from a suspension of belief, for if they cannot accept the common assumptions about the conduct of life, then they also refuse to posit other assumptions, or to declare contrary beliefs.

An impressive thesis can be made that the writer is a prime victim of the machine age or, more precisely, of the industrial society that is characterized by products that are made and consumed by the democratic masses. In *Against the American Grain*, Dwight Macdonald says: "For about two centuries Western culture has in fact been two cultures: the traditional kind—let us call it High Culture—that is chronicled in textbooks, and a novel kind that is manufactured for the market. This latter may be called

Mass Culture, or better Masscult, since it really isn't culture at all. . . . The question of Masscult is part of the larger question of the masses. The tendency of modern industrial society, whether in the USA or USSR, is to transform the individual into the mass man." Industrialization has accommodated the wide dissemination of the *kitschig* products that the masses admire and demand; in the arts, these are popular magazines, television, and, alas, books.

One can even speculate whether, given the pervasive verbal and visual aspects of the machine age, the artist will henceforth be able to create anything at all. In *The Image or What Happened to the American Dream*, Daniel Boorstin suggests that as technology keeps multiplying the objects that cozzen us, we find it difficult to engage the *real* world and to undergo *real* experience. He describes this dilemma as one resulting from our preference for images and for the illusions they project, rather than for direct personal experience. "We have used our wealth, our literacy, our technology, and our progress to create a thicket of unreality which stands between us and the facts of life. . . . The artificial has become so commonplace that the natural begins to seem contrived. The natural is the 'un—' and the 'non—.' . . . Fact itself has become '*non*fiction.' " The danger, it may be argued, is that the huge, homogenized public of the machine age is all too willing to accept the dictum that whatever is numerous and popular must be also good and true.

Now, no sensible person is unaware, or in some degree unresentful, of the conformity and standardization that so typifies contemporary life, nor can he avoid wondering at times whether he has not become the victim of some lunatic mechanistic scheme whose main object is to train him, as David Riesman and Mary McCarthy have variously said, to become a consumer. Little more can be done about the machine age, perhaps, but to treat it as a great historical comedy, or at the least, as Margaret Fuller concluded on her relations with the universe, to accept it. Still, it seems to me that we cannot accept something if we misrepresent it to ourselves, especially if we rely on misapplications of history. There is, for example, a recurrence of that old pathetic fallacy that the machine is anti-individual. Machines are conceptually unindividual; no machine was ever created to perform a single operation just once, yet that in itself hardly makes machines anti-human. There is, too, the tendency to regard the most essential consequences of technology as being modern, when actually a case can be made that men "lost" control over their movements—natural rhythms—as individuals with the invention of mechanical clocks, an event that took place long before the industrial society got into high gear.

It has, in fact, become popular to think of ourselves objectively as victims, as if we were somehow apart from our own terrors. The result of this kind of self-indulgence is never enlightening. On the popular level, for instance, Vance Packard has systematically exposed the fact that society is organized; and there are repeated exposés of contemporary schooling that inexorably reach the conclusion that universal education is not universally excellent. No social criticism of this sort is relevant unless it takes into account the choices that people have made, and are still making, among the things that society should do first, and abandon last. We have, for example, accepted the idea that some things must be sacrificed to the liberal credo that all people have a right to expect to live without the misery of physical deprivation. A fulfillment of that historical tenet is dependent upon making available to the masses a variety of sophisticated goods at a cheap price— and *that* is done by producing things in repeated forms and in great quantities. One ends by weighing sensibility and presumed necessity, and by relating common sense to individual sense. One looks at a thousand identical houses in an English "new town" and reflects that aesthetically one of them would have been enough, but one does not then logically conclude that the inhabitants are worse off than they were elsewhere.

At the worst, the argument that modern industrial life blunts the sensibility of the writer (or anyone else) lapses into sentimentality. At its best, it is a current manifestation of literary romanticism, a longing for what Perry Miller called "the sublime in America." Daniel

Boorstin feels a typical nostalgia. "We are deceived and obstructed by the very machines we make to enlarge our vision. In an earlier age, an architectural symbol of small-town, growing America was the friendly front porch. In our day, the architectural symbol is the picture window. . . . When we look out of our picture window . . . we are apt to see our neighbor himself. But he too is apt to be doing nothing more than looking at us through *his* picture window." Such contrivances, in short, leave us with ourselves—like the Hollywood love triangle which consists of an actor, his wife, and himself. Yet time has not only lent Boorstin a strange enchantment, it has also played dirty tricks on him. That fusty front porch was hardly a place to dispel illusion. You have only to read Sherwood Anderson to realize what horror was kept behind its friendly façade.

It is not, of course, sentimentality that most seriously informs our view of how we can be estranged from the modern age. We *expect* more than we have received from our having made the choices for the good life. We may have, still, a lingering view of the sublime possibility of America. F. Scott Fitzgerald said it: ". . . for a transitory enchanted moment man must have held his breath in the presence of this continent, compelled into an aesthetic contemplation he neither understood nor desired, face to face for the last time in history with something commensurate to his capacity for wonder." The key word here is "aesthetic." Again and again, the American writer has displayed a sense of just aggrievement that something was lost, needlessly, pointlessly, and that the vision of our authentically innocent past has not been vouchsafed. One of his characteristic moods is a haunting, brooding sense of disappointment. Few Europeans, with *their* history, have it. It is the romantic vision that admits the celebration of the simple life of nature, or tries to ascribe to simply physical activity the power of expiation, as in Whitman and Hemingway. Our conception of *place*—where we live or where we flee from—is predominantly aesthetic. (We ignore, for instance, the fact that the machine did not in terms of human accommodation radically disfigure the United States and Canada, nor, for that matter, Germany, France, and Russia, whatever it may have done to the green midlands of England. Practically every traveler to the United States of a century ago was appalled by the miserable little towns he saw on the Ohio, and affronted by the harshness of the prairie.) Indeed, it is hard to recollect what are the simple skills we are supposed to have lost as a result of the advent of industrialism and its ugly agent, mass production. The truth is that there is not much to recollect. "Before men showed off new cars, they showed off new horses," writes Mary McCarthy; "it is alleged against modern man that he as an individual craftsman did not make the car, but his grandfather did not make the horse either." I cannot feel abashed that Thoreau made his pencils by hand.

The critic John W. Aldrich, in reviewing a book by Alan Sillitoe, suggests that the novelists who were formerly known as "angry young men" ought, in their choice of subjects, to advance themselves from the lower-class life. Typically, they have depicted the frustrated and aimlessly rebellious young workingman who perceives that something is wrong with British society but holds forth no particular prescriptions for it. They should, suggests Aldrich, get on to other subjects and thus take a broader view. For a mixture of reasons, this is not a suggestion that could be made to the young American novelist, and the chief reason is, I think, that the working class as a proportionately large and socially identifiable segment of our society is all but disappearing. The most pervasive effect of advanced industrialism is to obliterate class distinctions of a traditional kind. During the past quarter-century an immense middle class has emerged, comprising perhaps seventy per cent of the population of the United States. The delineation between classes has progressively blurred, and the movement of people upward, while it continues, no longer involves a dramatic bursting through barriers, as it once did. The upper class is disappearing as a purely *social* class, and more and more is to be identified by the powers it holds (institutional powers—industrial, military, governmental, educational) rather than by the material possessions that once allowed it cultivated leisure. The generic middle class now includes skilled and semiskilled laborers, who actually have little in common with the hard core of the poor in America. Indeed, the "hard core of the poor" is a newly visible social phenomenon, for it has seemingly not diminished proportionately as the national prosperity has expanded, and it shows small evidence of the rapid change that we have always credited to American social classes. What may distinguish contemporary life in America today is the difference between the large mass of people who are prosperous to one degree or another and the smaller mass who are wholly unprosperous.

If this generally describes what has happened to American class structure under the impact of advancing industrialism, then it has great relevance to writing and to what writers write about. Class structure, for the novelist, is one of the social phenomena that define experience; and the interplay between classes can be said to *create* experience. Class is a form of reality that the novelist draws on, as did Henry James and Edith Wharton on the elegant old upper class; Theodore Dreiser and Sinclair Lewis on the middle class of the small town; James T. Farrell and William Saroyan on the immigrant working classes; Willa Cather and Thomas Wolfe on the lower middle class of the country town; William Faulkner on all the classes of a historically and geographically isolated region. For the novelist, class provides a point of view from which he may look down or up, or, rather, the vantage from which his characters do.

In a society that has a defined and perceivable class structure, in which more literate people are different from each other than are like each other, the writer may find himself alienated from his own class, or he may be in opposition to another class, but it is difficult to see how he can be alienated from the *whole* of society. Yet if, as seems to be happening in the United States in the second half of the twentieth century, society is becoming one huge class, then it is possible that an intellectual could find himself estranged from the composite, and homogenized, life of the whole. The social critic is today in the peculiar position of making judgments that apply to practically everyone, including himself. The relevance of this hypothesis on modern social organization is that as the years go on, young writers are likely to share more radically similar biographies, being for the most part products of middle-class upbringing, of suburban living, and of a vast educational process that leads from elementary school to high school to university. I do not see how it is possible to contemplate—as we are plainly doing now—the eventuality that everyone who has the capacity to learn will go to college without at the same time recognizing that this will create a conformity of experience among not only readers but also writers.

If the ultimate consequence of an advanced industrial society is to create a single class, then it will inevitably diminish the ideological conflicts in everyday life. When we complain about the "pressure to conform," about the sameness forced upon us by the products made for mass consumption, and when we fear that we will supinely accept the "images" that are projected by government, industry, and all the other agencies of mass democracy, we may in effect be saying, simply, that we are more like each other than we really care to be, though we may not surmise it, and that we got this way by the unmysterious condition of our growing up in practically the same way. For the writer—unless he believes with the older critics that sharing the same *terms* of life makes for a desirable coherent sensibility—this is a condition of no small significance. Unless, having escaped the middle class, he can lead an adventurous, or, better, a picaresque, life, as Hemingway did, there is not much experience he is likely to have with "other" people. Being together in Europe with other intellectuals and artists is not, for the American, being with other people. It becomes more difficult to lead a picaresque life, especially as we live in a time of peace. James Jones and Norman Mailer obviously *miss* war—as writers. Irwin Shaw stopped writing about war and, among similar works, produced *Lucy Crown,* which is about the sexual brutalization of a middle-class woman. War, in its own way, provides a kind of reality based on differences of biography: there is the immediately relevant difference between officers and men, but also, in a wartime setting, everyone is viewed as having come from somewhere else and as having been, before, someone else.

If one perceives real experience by means of an aesthetic judgment of the differences between people, and of the conflict between their values, then the writer will look away from those people who are like himself and seek situations where there are *other* people. (Or he may, indeed, look at himself at a time when *he* was different, a possibility that accounts, I think, for so much contemporary fiction and drama having to do with childhood.) The life of the poor and the dispossessed is real enough, but it cannot be perceived truly if in fact it is avoidable. George Orwell, when he descended into the lower depths of Paris and London, learned much about the down-and-out that he had previously only surmised, yet he was himself aware that his perceptions were limited by the ever-present possibility that he could escape, and this limitation was more restrictive than his natal middle-classness. Even though he was a volunteer in the Spanish Civil War, his experiences there were of a different order, for there was no way out, morally. Norman Mailer's seeking to become, to use his term, a "white Negro" acknowledges the strong compulsion in contemporary writing to comprehend the "other" life.

Should other avenues be closed, there is for the writer always the possibility of exploring the most elemental experiences of people just like himself, and this has, in many instances, come to mean an examination of their sexual experiences. Brutal life is the ordinary condition of the poor, the dispossessed: it is the primordial, antecedent condition of the materially affluent and the socially settled, who regard sexual intimacy as an unmistakable way to assert themselves and to commit others. Sexual mores are even used, in the hands of John O'Hara, to define the differences among people who cannot be shown to be different in other ways. In *Ten North Frederick,* the Irish politician's wife and daughter are nice people, not Lesbian, like the visitor to the Anglo-Saxon old-family Mrs. Chapin, and they would never go about getting wantonly pregnant, like Mrs. Chapin's daughter. Indeed, the preoccupation with sex as *evidence* of personality has a peculiarly middle-class bias. In the contemporary novel, too often the only way that a middle-class character asserts himself is sexually, unless he is made to turn to crime, or unless he is put directly in a setting of professional sports, where life is presumed to be "real."

If the attention to sex as a subject in so many modern novels is in fact derived from an obsessive interest in the brutal life, then it has to be related to the question of what experiences seem meaningful to a writer who thinks himself alienated from society. It provides conflict, it shows and makes a difference. There are other things to write about, obviously, but it is insensitive to conclude that the novelist who writes about sex is being perverse, or that he is limited emotionally and is merely seeking sensation. On the other hand, one can recognize that sex is a limited subject to work with. If writers do not recognize this, then readers will. The novelty of reading about sex wears off, and one soon finds that it no longer provides a shock of recognition but only a certain tiresomeness. Sexual love is too comical in its nature to bear much philosophizing. (The free circulation of Frank Harris's autobiography has probably done a great deal to reduce the prurient interest of readers in the candid description of sexual conquests: Harris's accounts are so gauche, so romantic, and so plainly funny that his life begins to seem like a Boucicault play performed at Minsky's.) An attention to incidences of sex in our lives and times is rapidly becoming the most boring aspect of contemporary writing, and whatever it may mean to the contemporary novelist, it will mean less and less to the reader. As in anything that is obvious, the more that is said, the less can be perceived. And yet, the fascination of the brutal life that so largely, over the past two decades, has characterized the newer novel must mean something to the observer. In the mirror of serious fiction, we see more of ourselves than we care to credit.

On Selling, Like Say,
Francis Bacon

Selling, you might say, is the practice of imparting information and of persuading others to act upon it. You might
say, but nobody believes it. Thorstein Veblen, for
example, thought that selling depends on that "range of
human infirmities which bear fruit in psychopathic
wards," which does not say very much for buyers, either.
Though choleric, Veblen was logical, for he did say that
buying is generally a conspicuous expenditure; that makes
of selling a disposable expense. Then there was Bruce
Barton, the noted adman and hagiographer, who found
Jesus to be The Greatest Salesman in History, followed by
lesser figures on the order of Napoleon and Disraeli.
Between these viewpoints there is a range of not very distinguished commentary on selling, but it is not my purpose here to embark, like Cyrano on his nose, on a
gasconade—selling philosophic, selling economic, selling psychologic, etc., etc.

Rather, as a former traveler, I want simply to impress on laymen that selling trade books, particularly, is hard work. The fact is that everyone respects books but few people buy them. For the salesman this means that while his wares are prized he is himself without support. Self-sacrifice is readily learned in the book business, as in a certain firm when the binding glue on some sample copies of a geography text gave off an offensive odor and salesmen were instructed to say to customers, "Ma'am, if you smell something, it's not the book, it's me." Hardly more can be asked of an American. What the good salesman needs to begin with is a combination of raw energy and fine feelings; what he ends with is the enfeebling of the one and the coarsening of the other. His burden is to be opposite himself, and never of a piece. If he is knowledgeable then he must appear unspoiled by learning, and if he is intent on business he must seem as casual as comfort. The salesman lives by small talk, like someone at a cocktail party where there are only strangers and no chairs, but he is not expected to bore others with irrelevancies. He cannot, like the rest of us, ask whether the hippopotamus is a male or female when in fact the answer cannot conceivably interest anyone but another hippopotamus.

In every book salesman there is something of the actor, and still more of the eighteenth-century letter writer who assumed that even occasional acquaintance merits the courtesy of practiced expression. Few salesmen, admittedly, master the grand manner, like Abe Burrows when he escorted guests to an elevator and commanded the operator to "take these people wherever they want to go," but then again, writers do not furnish salesmen with lines, but with books, most of which are neither grand nor funny. Inevitably the book salesman is a gossip, for publishing is the natural field for the cultivation of interesting misinformation. "No man is exempt from saying silly things," to misquote a writer, "but the salesman's lot is to say them deliberately."

Out of a want of pride, and maybe a hurt sensibility, book salesmen sometimes, in the old days, tried to disguise themselves by the use of elegant variations like "bookman" and "publisher's representative." That they did not read Fowler is obvious. What is less obvious is that they did not read much at all, by intention. It was a publishing axiom that a salesman is most effective and least inhibited when offering a book he has not read, and he need not apologize, for

> *What's Taylor Caldwell to him or*
> *he to Taylor Caldwell,*
> *That he should weep for her?*

Anyway, it is not reading but observation that is the salesman's first talent, and it is this that makes him cynical. A seasonal reassessment of one's friends is enough to turn any sensible man into a skeptic. Fall after spring, year upon year, the salesman observes his customers as they grow long in discourse and short of memory, and he comes to realize that it is more blessed to listen than to talk. That very experience tends to make salesmen take short cuts in the daily discourse, like one I know who asks even a new customer how his wife's back is, on the generally infallible grounds that any man over forty has a wife with a bad back.

Such generalizations, however informed, do not prove that a salesman is wiser than the rest of us. Wisdom does not occur in people by profession, despite the popular myth that it is given to travelers. Truck drivers are not to be trusted in picking places to eat, and taxi drivers are not only boring conversationalists but also unreliable ones, being full of half-heard remarks. A book salesman is not likely to understand the human condition any better than you and I, though he is probably less impressed by old jokes and jibes than I am, for he has been this way and, unlike Elizabeth Browning's mortal traveler, he will pass this way again.

Going Downtown

Not long ago the financial community, as it calls itself in a vaguely utopian way, discovered book publishing. For investors it became a popular "new" industry like electronics or plastics. During a period of three years ending in 1962, owners of publishing houses were offered the chance to "go public," that is, to convert their proprietorship into shares that would be traded (and priced) on the stock market. The result was that many of them turned from their more or less obscure pursuit of gain to the open market of public finance where, they were to learn, money is handled with a certain *élan* if also with less realism. However profitable this may have been for publishers, it is hard to know what possessed Wall Street, for obviously it had overestimated the immediate prospects of a relatively small industry. In time the possession passed and publishing stocks fell precipitously. No doubt the decline affected a number of investors who, as Oscar Wilde said of men and women in marriage, entered into an alliance because they were either tired or curious and were in both cases disappointed. It was up and it was down. And for the publisher it was strange to be so abruptly exalted and deprecated, yet it *was* an experience and, accepting at least one premise of modern fiction, it is a good thing to have an experience.

Before a company is allowed to place its shares for public sale it must take part in a curious tribal rite known as the "due diligence meeting," attendance at which is required by the Securities and Exchange Commission of all novitiates in the stock market. One is supposed to have exercised "due diligence" in making known the nature and proclivities of his enterprise. I recall that meeting with what may properly be called mixgivings. Not realizing that it was a formal, if not a solemn, occasion, I came downtown without a prepared address. I began my impromptu remarks with the subject of the scandalous piracy by nineteenth-century American publishers of the works of Charles Dickens and Mrs. Trollope and others of their English contemporaries. Then I passed—though it can hardly have been gracefully or even consequentially—to the nature of present-day publishing, and at last concluded by reflecting that, were it not already in use, that singular phrase "almost never" would certainly have been invented by Wall Street traders. Having exercised some degree of diligence, if not of caution, I went back uptown. Two weeks later the stock opened at twenty-three dollars and fifty cents. Later it was selling at forty dollars. Success doth make cowards of us all, and especially of the newly rich. Nowadays I speak to investors formally: that is quite enough about Mrs. Trollope.

Book publishing is an excellent industry in which to invest money, but who can venture how much one should invest, or when? (I once asked the broker James Rich when was the best time to buy stocks. "When you have the money," he said.) Generalization is deceptive, given the idiosyncrasies of publishers. One can speak only for himself in answering the questions that investors frequently put to publishers. What is being done in research and development? What is the future of teaching machines? Will paperbacks render hard-cover books obsolete? Will a few large firms dominate the book business?

Research and development is one of those oracular phrases that promise more than they mean: it sounds engagingly scientific even when applied to matters that cannot be weighed or measured. In a large manufacturing business there is reason for the existence of a separate department given to research. In a publishing house, however, such a department would be superfluous. A good publisher's main business is research in, or receptivity to, ideas, no less than the encouragement and development of talent. This is at once the germ and the fruit of his effort.

In a single year a publisher may include in his list as many as eight "first" novelists. Probably he will lose money on each book, but consider that John Updike and J. D. Salinger were once "first" novelists. The writer must begin somewhere; so must the publisher. Before *By Love Possessed* James Gould Cozzens published eleven novels and each of them was, although moderately profitable to both the author and publisher, antecedent to one of the largest-selling books of the twentieth century. A publisher ought, in short, to harness contradictory qualities by gambling patiently. Not everything, it hardly needs to be said, issued from American publishing houses is the result of a worthy risk, nor is it literature. There are numerous "made" or "packaged" books that are conceived and produced for people who really do not read. One recognizes them instantly and conveniently by their titles—*Sexual Satisfaction in Marriage, How to Take Ten Strokes Off Your Golf Game, Pictures of the Civil War*. To specialize in such books is neither interesting nor responsible publishing, nor is it in the long run steadily profitable. There is an aphorism, so worn it has become a cliché, that one ought to publish authors and not single books. Fine houses adhere to this principle in the main, and while they publish general lists that include popular books that will scarcely endure the season, they also devote themselves to criticism, history, poetry, drama, and serious fiction by young writers.

Into such books goes a publisher's search and from them comes an eventual profit. A backlist of hundreds or thousands of titles will sell steadily year after year. It will, moreover, bring in a higher rate of profit than new books because the "starting-up" cost of older titles has long since been amortized and expensed. As much as sixty per cent of a trade (or general-book) publisher's current sales can be derived from his backlist, which includes all titles in print that are more than a year old. For example, each of Sinclair Lewis's major novels sells on an average three thousand copies a year, with no expenditure on advertising or promotion, and this sale from titles that were originally published more than thirty-five years ago is quite apart from the considerable revenues derived from paperback editions. Not every publisher enjoys the sustenance of such a backlist, nor, conversely, is everyone sensible to the necessity of close budgeting on new titles. So it is that the average trade publisher would show a net loss at year's end were it not for the proceeds he gains from the sale of subsidiary rights to his books—income from book clubs and paperback reprints mainly—or what is ironically known in the trade as "other income."

The usual inquiry about research and development is not made to the general book publisher, of course, but to the textbook publisher who is concerned with a more predictable audience than prevails for trade books, an audience that is defined, indeed circumscribed, by institutional systems. Schools and colleges create courses of study for which certain kinds of textbooks are needed, and the publisher is expected not only to fulfill present needs but to anticipate new ones. In both expectations he is informed and sustained by the particular nature of American education which, to use Henry Adams's phrase, is governed by the principle of acceleration.

The American, who likes to regard himself as Crève-cœur saw him, as the new man, would seem to renew himself not only by changing his environment but also by improving his means of learning about environment. We are a people who trust to education, and have done so from the beginning. America was in a unique measure founded by educated men—how many Cambridge men were trading with the Indians in 1630?—who recognized that the first necessity was not to glorify their good fortune but to increase it by provision and use. An astonishingly large proportion of American social and political ideas has been devoted to education. Even the American radical—Henry George, Eugene Debs, Thorstein Veblen—has tended to believe that social evils arise not so much from man's neglect of other men but of himself, of his ability, through learning, to control his environment—the greatest vested interest is not property but ignorance. The American rich now leave their harvests to education, creating libraries and scholarships and laboratories rather than endowing religious orders or erecting *Hofburgs*. If one comes to equate social progress with education, then he will in some degree accept the peculiarly indigenous philosophy of William James and John Dewey, the pragmatic philosophy that holds that knowledge ought to increase speculation about the real rather than the unreal (a contrast, if you will, between the scientific and the religious forms of experience).

Given this tradition of attempting to educate the whole of society, which in the past decade has been intensified for reasons of international competition, the American publisher can anticipate an almost unlimited market for educational books. It seems likely that this market will grow at a rate of fifteen per cent a year during the next decade, far faster than the rate of population growth. The profound motivation of our adherence to the educational idea suggests that the demand for books and other teaching materials cannot be seriously diverted or lessened by the vagaries of business trends or cycles. Is such optimism in itself typically American? I suppose so. Whether or not he accepts this view, the responsible textbook publisher will perceive that his market is not only growing but changing.

Some of the ways in which we learn about our environment have already been transformed. The arithmetic and mathematics of a decade ago have largely given way to new techniques and concepts, and the parent of a fourth-grade child finds himself embarrassed by the simplest homework. There is the possibility, too, that we shall alter drastically the approach to learning our language. It seems probable that the conventional "prescriptive" grammar and syntax that have been part of the school and college curriculum for the past half-century will now be largely abandoned in favor of the more accurate and more extensive descriptions of the English language that emerge from the scholarship of Whitehall, Fries, and others. Now a publisher can, of course, wait for someone to submit a manuscript that renders the new linguistics into a readily teachable form. He will do better to commission and help direct the writing of such a work, and thus perform the kind of research that is made practicable by his close relation to scholars and teachers.

The textbook publisher has several means of access to the schools and colleges. His salesmen call upon thousands of institutions in the ordinary drill of their duties. Their primary duty is to sell books, yet by the very nature of their product, and by the inclination of their customers, they gather significant information on the trends of educational courses and so inform the editors of textbooks, who are ultimately responsible for whatever publishing may contribute to the advancement of education. It is, admittedly, a nice course that the editor must steer between the sometimes too rigid choices of advanced scholarship and conventional teaching. The editor who looks at five competing books and then with the aid of a compliant author produces a sixth book accomplishes something, not much but something: he will have published a book that immediately is outdated as well as secondhand and second-rate. Too many textbooks are made this way, and the most convincing proof of imitation, though perhaps the least harmful result of it, is the persistence of factual errors from book to book, from revision to revision. Martin Mayer in an article in *Harper's Magazine* mentions that "elementary texts dealing with geography typically teach the nonsense of 'frigid, temperate, and torrid zones,' which has been out of date for roughly four centuries. (There is no point along the Equator nearly so hot as Death Valley, which is in the 'temperate zone,' and much of the Arctic never gets as cold as Missoula, Montana.)" A responsible editor will maintain a curiosity about ideas in education and will, however slowly or painfully, attempt to persuade his employers to risk, experiment, and improvise. Yet even in his boldest moments he will also be sufficiently realistic, and literate enough, to recognize that the function of textbooks is to *introduce* students to the disciplines of learning.

The choices are not always as hard or contrary as I have suggested, nor is an editor forever engaged in examining the goals of education. He is, in fact, more often concerned with improving the techniques of his craft. The most important single thing in publishing is the English sentence, and the editor who cannot contemplate it again and again with a sense of wonder has not yet gained respect for the complexity of learning. (The English sentence becomes the French sentence in France, but it should remain the English sentence in the United States. One is appalled by the recent suggestion of the Mayor of New York City that Spanish-speaking immigrants from Puerto Rico should not be required to learn English in order to pass certain public examinations. This is liberalism gone mushy, a tolerant conviction that everyone has a right to be handicapped.) Much is made these days of "communication" and "the language arts," but such jargon is the luxury of school administrators, not of editors, who are constantly confronted with the necessity to make clear and accurate the basic units of meaning. This is, no doubt, too rigorous and elemental a view, but one likes to recall that Gibbon said that once he got right the first sentence of *The Decline and Fall of the Roman Empire* the rest followed.

Teaching machines seem to have lit the imagination of a number of investors in publishing houses, not alone because gadgetry appeals but possibly because there persists the suspicion that books are neither as cheap nor as convenient as they might be. Following World War I it was anticipated that motion-picture films would become important in the classroom, but this was too sanguine. Films were expensive; the equipment was cumbersome;

the old Celluloid reels were flammable. Soon after World War II the hope for an expanded, even dominant, use of audio-visual materials rested on the availability, in addition to films, of the less costly media of filmstrips, recordings, tapes, and overhead projectors. None of these devices has become a *main* means of teaching in the schools and colleges, nor has any seriously affected the currency of textbooks. Next came educational television, which is perhaps the most publicized and most mishandled learning device of our time and one that may barely survive at the hands of its supporters. Consider the consequence when an airplane commissioned by the Ford Foundation flew over an Indiana town in order to telecast teaching sessions to three Midwestern states: thousands of teachers had to interrupt their regular schedules in order to accommodate it. A solution to that particular annoyance was found in broadcasting prerecorded programs on a less rigorous schedule, but of course it was hardly necessary to employ aircraft in order to make "canned" teaching films available to schools. The inflexibility of educational television is to be seen, too, in the instruction of students at home. Harcourt, Brace was the first publisher, so far as I know, to issue a textbook for a home television course (Professor Frank C. Baxter's "Shakespeare on TV" at the University of Southern California in 1954), and it soon discovered how difficult it is to prepare teaching materials for persons who are inaudible and, in effect, unknown.

Most recently the teaching machine has won supporters, some of whom have persisted in confusing the mechanical object itself with the technique of learning that is known as "programing." In 1958 I talked with Professor B. F. Skinner, of Harvard, about his work with paper discs (and tapes) that were designed to move past a little window in a machine and reveal to a student hundreds of simple questions in a sequential order. The subject being presented—a college psychology course, in one instance, or English spelling—was fragmented, as it were, into very small and easily comprehended learning steps, with the result that as the student gave his answers (recorded on a separate tape in the machine) the chances of their being incorrect were slight and the student's inducement to learn—or, in Skinner's terminology, his reinforcement or "reward"—was continual. Later Harcourt, Brace commissioned the construction of a more complex machine than Skinner's earlier one and at the same time engaged Joseph C. Blumenthal to write a "program" (that is, a block of subject matter broken down into a sequence of small learning steps) that was to be printed on tape for use on the machine. Still later Harcourt, Brace abandoned its experiments with machinery and, having on its hands Blumenthal's completed program on English syntax and grammar, published the program as a book, *English 2600*, naming it after the number of teaching questions it contained. Several years later this remains, in schools, the most widely used single product of the teaching-machine era.

Enough time has elapsed, I should think, to evaluate publishers' experience with teaching machines and programed learning. The machines themselves have tended to be either cumbersome and expensive or almost pointlessly simple and fragile. Placed in a separate room of a school, a battery of machines requires superintending by teachers, and this can be onerous as well as self-defeating, because it takes teachers out of classrooms. Placed within a classroom the teaching machine is really out of context, for it is not a *group* learning device; no two students will proceed through a program at the same pace, and there is no provision for the teacher to guide and implement the learning of several students simultaneously. Interestingly, while most exponents of programed learning have regarded it as essentially a tutorial device, a means for a student to learn by himself, one of its best uses *in book form* may be in group learning. Mrs. Paul Roberts, of the Overseas School of Rome, has achieved fine results by leading a class through a program, now and again stating the answers to printed questions herself or calling for answers from individual students after having discussed some phase of the subject.

Of course, the innovation that Professor Skinner and others have brought about is not in the creation of machines but in the creation of programed learning, the

presentation of information and concepts in certain logically perceivable patterns. While the teaching machine
may prove to have a role as a tutorial device in the home
(although I myself doubt this), its *method* of teaching seems
to be best presented in the classroom in book form. Even
here technological advancements are needed. Most programed books are still designed with six or eight "frames"
on a page, that is, outlined spaces for type that are perhaps
an inch deep and four inches wide; the frames are a
descendant of the little windows on the teaching machines,
not unlike the buggy-whip holders on the first automobile
carriages. Some way must be found to conserve space on
the page, for a major drawback of programed books is
their costly production. Quite apart from technics, perhaps the most serious mistake that publishers made
when they first undertook programs was to ignore the
principles of sound publishing. They were importuned to
believe that programing was best achieved by allying a
writer, a teacher, an editor, and a psychologist to produce
a single program; yet we all should know that committees
do not write good books. A programed book can be no
less than a book.

While it is not likely that there is a secure place for
the teaching machine in American schools and colleges,
audio-visual devices are not necessarily compromised by
this. The development of "language laboratories" has, for
example, been a major advance in the teaching of foreign

languages to students at all age levels. Projectors of all kinds are becoming more convenient and inexpensive to use, as are tape recorders. Yet the fact is that such devices are ancillary to the main medium for teaching, which is printed expository prose. The book is a marvelously efficient device: portable, durable, inexpensive, and adapted for use by one person or by a various number in communication with each other.

Even the paperback is not a startling new device. A paperback is a book with a paper cover. Perhaps the simplest way to suggest the relationship between paperback and hard-cover books—and to clarify the common misconception that publishers somehow are withholding great savings from the public by persisting to issue the latter—is to recount the idle threats one hears from some paperback publishers who declare that if hard-bound publishers do not cease asking for high advances on the reprint licenses to their books, then the paperback publishers will be forced to publish original works themselves and, so to speak, do away with a greedy middleman. This is no threat at all. No publisher can prevent others from publishing, nor would he wish to. Very few new authors have been published originally in low-priced paperback form with success, for such books cannot be issued in safe, small printings, and the whole rationale of *inexpensive* paperback publishing depends upon books being printed in huge lots for distribution to tens of thousands of retail outlets. The publisher of the inexpensive paperback volume is for the most part a *reprint* publisher: he issues in a different and cheaper format a book that was accorded either respect or popularity, or both, on its original publication. He gambles, naturally, but his is a different kind of risk-taking from that of the hard-bound publisher. He gambles on large printings—and this is a large risk, for there is practically no "remaindering," or reselling at a reduced price, of paperback books—and he risks the probability that many of his titles will be accorded little display space in the drugstores, air terminals, newsstands, and places other than bookstores where books are sold. For him, in addition to all this, to finance a "first" novel or a book of criticism, for example, is to multiply his present risks and to add unfamiliar ones.

There is no reason why a publisher cannot profitably publish both hard-bound and paper-bound books, as indeed many publishers do, but the tendency in such instances is to publish higher-priced paperbacks which are sold mainly to the same retailers as hard-bound books, that is, to bookstores. Such paperbacks are, for the most part, reprints; their status has already been established by earlier publication and because of this they are accorded very little promotion or advertising, which accounts in good part for their being cheaper than hard-bound books. The production costs of paper-bound books are little understood in the publishing business itself. There is actually only a small saving in costs in using paper to cover a book *unless* the book is also printed in a tight format on cheap paper and *unless* it is also "perfect bound," a harmlessly spurious term for a technique of imperfect binding in which the pages are merely glued to the cover and are not, therefore, sewn together and attached, by a fairly costly operation, to cover "boards." On a four-dollar textbook that is *not* "perfect bound" but is sewn to make it considerably more durable (though not as durable as if it had boards), the saving on board and cloth is only about twenty-five cents. While the saving to the customer then would be about eighty cents (allowing for the publisher's markup), the resulting volume would have but a fifth or sixth the lifetime of a carefully made hard-bound volume.

Indeed, a publisher of a paper-bound textbook can readily profit from its lack of durability, for not only must the textbook be replaced frequently but it will also have practically no resale value. It should not be necessary, by now, to explain that publishers do not have a secret vested interest in hard-bound textbooks, that paperback books are more expensive for students and schools to buy for basic courses, whatever other virtues they possess. Quite apart from the question of cost and price, paperback books can give to the elementary and secondary schools and to the colleges a remarkable variety and richness of reading. Many conventional textbooks are at the same time too elaborate and too restrictive. Paperbacks can, in contrast, lend to teaching materials a greater range and become, as it were, multiple and extensible instruments of learning. In any event, the question is not one of opposing paperbacks to hard-bound books, but of adding one to the other: what the development of paperback publishing has accomplished is to increase reading, to proliferate the use of books, and to make all forms of publishing more profitable.

It is commonplace, if also wearisome, to speak of "image," the image the public holds of an institution or the image of a product created in the minds of buyers under the stimulus of advertising. This is a concept, I would assume, derived partly from Plato (the cave), partly from aesthetics and physiology (the optic), and partly from Freudian psychology. One may question whether it is a useful concept in the conduct of ordinary affairs. Does the public familiarly hold an image of publishing? I doubt that the public thinks about publishing at all. Not one reader in a thousand is able to identify the publisher of an important book if it is not being currently advertised, or, to be sure, even if it *is* being advertised. It is an exercise in vanity to become anxious over the possibility that the public will, because of the recent mergers among firms, come to regard book publishing as "big business" and will no longer respect it as a highly personal enterprise.

I am not at all certain that size in itself is relevant to sound publishing except as it may give broader opportunities to people of talent. A large publishing house can publish good books, and many a small publisher has devoted himself to poor ones. The danger is not that a few houses will come to dominate American publishing—this is improbable, if not wholly unreasonable, to suppose—but that the large publishing house will fail to accomplish the better ends to which great resources might be put. Already one perceives a slight case of elephantiasis in publishing firms, the symptoms of which are expediters, co-ordinators, consultants, and public-relations counselors, any one of whom may regrettably cost as much as a talented editor or designer. The small publisher is spared this disease and it is one of his strengths that he must depend on his own counsel. Now that the interest of Wall Street in publishing has subsided somewhat, there is less of a lure for the small publisher to seek a merger with a larger colleague. One publisher who had previously risen to the lure is now said to be wondering if there is some way in which one can "go private."

A Vision of Good
and Evil:
Part One

One night in March of 1962 Milovan Djilas and I walked
about Belgrade the whole night through. It was not yet
spring and the air was chill and wet. Earlier that day
Djilas had insisted that I buy a beret, his own favorite
headwear, to guard against the cold. "Why do you Americans never dress properly against bad weather?" he asked,
and when I suggested that it was possibly so because we
are a people who expect to move on, he disagreed,
laughing. "No, it is because you expect to conquer even
the elements." The streets of Belgrade are dreary enough
during the daytime; at night they are desolate and, on
those few avenues that are lighted nakedly in the modern
fashion, they appear rather pathetic, as if greater things
had been expected. We walked several times through the
gardens across from the Hotel Metropole past the ocher-
colored Orthodox church, and then down the Bulevar
Revolucije to the Moše Pijade, where the Communist

party invests rather stark buildings with great flat concrete forms of blank walls and windows. Finally we came to Kalemegdan, the old Turkish fortress overlooking the confluence of the Danube and the Sava. Here we talked for several hours, strolling along with that typically interrupted motion of conversationalists who must pause to make a point.

Politics, Djilas said, is the face put upon philosophy: we do not easily recognize some ideas unless they are given expression in the policies and programs of governments and parties. He has what I should prefer to think is a pre-twentieth-century notion that politics represents an inquiry into man's capacity and his will to act outside himself and is, in this particular sense, a speculation on man's nature. He was, he said that night at Kalemegdan, turning more and more to the study of religion, though he was not himself a believer in revealed religion or a supporter of its organizations. "I respect religion as a form of truth, but there are many forms." Increasingly he was interested in exploring the question of dualism, of the opposition of forces or substances of good and evil, and he would like to comprehend the themes of Zoroaster as they appeared and reappeared among the Mithraic celebrants, the Manicheans, the Christian Gnostics, and, in Djilas's own homeland, the Bogomils. They might be comprehended in our own time as well. Perhaps we had during the twentieth century taken part in a Manichean struggle in the lives of men and nations. Hitler and Stalin had revealed the extraordinary power of evil that apparently is not reformed by history, nor by man's progress, but can emerge suddenly and wholly, as if willed by itself.

As I listened to Milovan Djilas I recognized in the political leader he had been, no less than in the writer he was, the effects of a split vision. He seemed persistently concerned with the conflict of opposites which he saw clearly, and painfully. Was it so, he appeared to ask, that the evil in us will not be overcome but that the good in us can never allow the reality of this and we must live by the myth of an ultimate goodness? Djilas's own experiences are uniquely those of a man who has wielded power and at the same time questioned the use of it. As a political leader he was oftentimes arbitrary and harsh, in the particular way of intellectuals, but he could also be impulsively warm and frequently humorous, like a man who had shared common hardships. In *Conversations with Stalin* he wrote, "I am, of course, far from thinking that success in political struggles is the only value. It especially does not occur to me to identify politics with amorality, though I do not deny that, by the very fact that politics involve a struggle for the survival of given human communities, they are thereby marked by a disregard for moral norms. For me great politicians and great statesmen are those who can join ideas and realities. . . ." The idea and the reality, the ideal and the result, the beginning and the end—these are implicit in every act, of course, but only rarely are they seen simultaneously, and for this a man needs the peculiar vision of a poet or a prophet.

Djilas has that kind of vision, and perhaps because of it he has at times acted with what appears to be caprice or footless confusion. At the height of his power, when he was second only to Tito in the Yugoslav regime, he publicly examined the nature of the oligarchy of bureaucrats he himself helped to create. Even foreign correspondents who are sympathetic to Djilas's plight have mistaken his tendency to hold in tandem opposite views as evidence of naïveté. During the examination of his heresy before the Parliament in 1954 he was at one point inclined, through a curious sense of sympathy for conformists who are faced by disbelief in their own leader, to vote for his own censure. At another time, during the trial that sent him to his present imprisonment, he behaved rebelliously, according to foreign observers, yet at the same time asked to be permitted to read the indictment against him. Such behavior may appear "undignified" to those who are merely looking on (and are not themselves about to be sentenced to nine years in prison for writing a book), but I think it is understandable in a man who is capable of both violent reaction to persecution and an intellectual interest in its official rationale.

If it is more than a cliché that twentieth-century man is tormented by a search for his identity, then Milovan

Djilas in his own person, as both a political leader and a writer, must dramatize the truth of it. "A man can abandon everything—home, country, land—but he cannot abandon himself," he has written. In his books, the very works that either led him to prison (*The New Class* and *Conversations with Stalin*) or were written during his confinement (*Montenegro, Njegoš,* and *The Leper and Other Stories*), Djilas has again and again sought to find his own identity by reflecting on the homeland from which he rose. In his vision, as in every writer's, there are scenes from the past.

I

Milovan Djilas was brought before the Belgrade district court in December of 1956 on the charge that, on the occasion of the Hungarian uprising of that year, he had published statements "slandering Yugoslavia." During the trial proceedings there occurred a brief exchange between the chief judge and the prisoner that seemed, to foreigners at least, strangely irrelevant. The chief judge, in giving the defendant's personal history, described him as a Montenegrin, whereupon Djilas, who bore the extravagant indictment and, still later, the pronouncement of a sentence of three years' "strict imprisonment" without discernible emotion, leaped to his feet. "I object," he declared. "The statement should show that I am a Yugoslav."

In the twentieth century it has become common for a man to be condemned by his own identity. The judge was hardly unaware that no more justly, or violently, proud people exist than the Montenegrins and that normally Milovan Djilas would declare his own pride. Yet the judge could, at that moment, imply that Djilas's fierce heredity impelled him against the Communist regime of Yugoslavia, that the heresy for which he was being tried was to be expected because it was inbred in him. Djilas had only recently been Vice-President of Yugoslavia and the newly elected President of its one-party Parliament, but now, the judge could suggest, these political experiences were less important than Djilas's own racial memories. His grandfather (and likely his father, too) was a rebel against the princes of Montenegro long before there existed a Yugoslav nation. Defiance was nothing new in a Montenegrin.

It is not unusual for the Yugoslav regime to dwell upon the distinctiveness of its several peoples, because Yugoslavia began, following World War I, as an uneasy alliance among four ethnic groups: Serbs, Croats, Slovenes, and Macedonians. To the north and the west live the Slovenes, and the numerically greater Croats (including the Croats who inhabit Dalmatia and parts of Bosnia). The Serb lands form a broad crescent in the east fronting the Slovenes and the Croats, with one point of the crescent on the border of Hungary to the north and the other

point touching the Adriatic to the southwest in Montenegro. To the south, in the center, and to the southeast,
are the Macedonians. The Serbians and Montenegrins are
one people ethnically and linguistically and, except for a
small Moslem minority, are almost wholly Orthodox.
They reflect still their Byzantine "eastern" past and, no
less, the influences left by the rule of the Ottoman Turks
before the nineteenth century. The Croatians and Slovenes are mostly Catholic—indeed, in the provinces of
Bosnia and Hercegovina the distinction between Serb and
Croat is entirely one of religion—and to their Catholicism
they may ascribe, as well as to their domination by
Austria-Hungary up to the time of World War I, their
"western" culture. The Macedonians are of mixed Serbian, Bulgarian, Greek—all Orthodox—and Albanian origin and were only superficially unified during the centuries of Turkish domination which left among them a
great many Moslems and left, as well, a host of political
factions that favored now Serbia, now Bulgaria, and
occasionally Greece.

Among these four ethnic groups there persist, though
progressively with less consequence, the disparate effects
of the past. Among them are not only three religions but
three languages: Serbo-Croatian (a single language with
two alphabets, Cyrillic and Latin), Slovene, and Macedonian—each Slavic and closely allied but different enough
to require the publication of Yugoslav books in four

editions. Among them, too, are the occasional political remains of the rise and fall of three Balkan empires, the medieval Serbian, the Ottoman, and the Austro-Hungarian.

It may be that one must deny history in order to make history. Certainly the present regime has reason not to emphasize the composite nature of Yugoslavia, for its history from 1919 to 1948 is a painful record of opposition, on religious and political grounds, between peoples who in fact have more to share than to dispute. It may not be fanciful to suppose that part of the Communist success in fostering unification is owed to the nice balance among its postwar leaders: Josip Broz-Tito is by birth a Croatian, Alexander Ranković a Serb, Edvard Kardelj a Slovene, and Milovan Djilas a Montenegrin. Even the Communist who would seek to change the ways of the past must accept the inevitability that all men carry the mark of their origins.

In his own past Milovan Djilas has at different times been a revolutionary, a soldier, a political leader, and always a writer. During the early part of the 1930's his journalistic writings and his work as a Communist organizer made him an enemy of the Yugoslav royal government. Twenty years later, in January of 1954, the publication of a series of newspaper articles led to his expulsion from the Yugoslav Communist party and his dismissal from office. He had undertaken to write a philosophical defense of Yugoslavia's "national" communism after Tito's break with Stalin in 1948, but within a few years, to the dismay of Tito, Djilas turned to an analysis and criticism of his own party.

Following his dismissal he passed a year under close police watch, jobless and alone but still engaged in writing, before he was brought to trial—the first of three trials during this period—in January of 1955. The charge was one of "hostile propaganda," arising from an interview he gave to the New York *Times*. Released on a suspended sentence, he returned to the Belgrade apartment where he lived with his wife and small son and there devoted the next two years to the writing of *The New Class* and *Land Without Justice*. The manuscripts of both books were completed before his imprisonment at Sremska Mitrovica, the Serbian state prison fifty miles from Belgrade, in December of 1956. This, his first imprisonment by the Communist regime, was ordered at his second trial, this time on charges of having "slandered Yugoslavia" in statements made to the foreign press. During October of 1957 he left his cell only long enough to be tried and sentenced a third time as a result of the publication in the United States of his book *The New Class*. After more than four years in prison—part of the time in solitary confinement—he was conditionally released in January of 1961. Fifteen months later he was once again arrested because of his writing. The publication of the book *Conversations with Stalin* led to a trial in May of 1962, the judgment of which returned him to Sremska Mitrovica under a sentence of eight years and eight months.

Milovan Djilas is there now, the world's most famous prisoner, for him a bleak and tragic distinction. While not presently in solitary confinement, he is denied writing materials, a deprivation that for him must constitute a negation of his being. "I have little material for the writing of history," he once wrote, "but I remember too much—and too much that is evil—to be able to keep silence. For I am myself from Montenegro, torn between the ideal and the reality."

II

"The revolution," writes Djilas in *Land Without Justice*, "gave me everything—except what I had idealistically expected from it." And what had he expected? The years of his manhood provided him with the grim test of heroism. During the German and Italian occupation of his country he faced death several times throughout three years of guerrilla warfare against the enemy—and these years had made of him both a respected soldier and a feared party leader. But he restlessly yearned for something more. "So it has always been here: one fights to achieve sacred dreams, and plunders and lays waste along the way—to live in misery, in pain and death, but in one's thoughts to travel far." He sought, and could not find in these times, the simple beauty of human justice. And in writing the biography of his early years, his search must carry him back to another and earlier time, when he was a boy and youth in Montenegro.

There is but a thin line between the heroic and the grotesque, as between tragedy and comedy, and quite naturally the few truly heroic peoples of the world have been viewed with humor as well as respect. The legend of Montenegro lends itself to both. In part, it reflects Gladstone's testament that "the traditions of Montenegro exceed in glory those of Marathon and Thermopylae and all the war traditions of the world," and Lord Tennyson's conclusion, in his sonnet "Montenegro":

> *O smallest among peoples! rough rock-throne*
> *Of Freedom! Warriors beating back the swarm*
> *Of Turkish Islam for five hundred years,*
> *Great Tzernagora! never since thine own*
> *Black ridges drew the cloud and brake the storm*
> *Has breathed a race of mightier mountaineers.*

In part, also, it reflects the many stories told, sometimes in malice but always with delight, of the Montenegrins' fondness for self-glorification and their unfailing instinct for excess. In the days of their princedom—its boundaries

embracing scarcely seventy-five square miles and no more
than a quarter of a million subjects—they spoke seriously
of themselves and the Russians as comprising a force of
"one hundred and sixty millions." After World War I, as
inductees in the newly created Yugoslav army, some
Montenegrins refused to follow the customary "count
off" of soldiers in the line on the grounds that no Montenegrin could be expected publicly to declare himself
"second" or "third." Instead, he might sing out "first
after the first" or "first after the first after the first."

As conspirators the Montenegrins are no less eccentric, as Fitzroy Maclean suggests in his biography of Tito.
In 1940 Josip Broz-Tito, then secretary-general of the out-
lawed and hunted Communist party in Yugoslavia, summoned party leaders to a secret conference at a house
outside of Zagreb. "All went well except that an overzealous lookout man opened fire on the Montenegrin
delegation, who, with the careless enthusiasm of their race,
had mislaid their instructions." The lookout man is not
identified by Maclean, but somehow one senses that he,
too, was a Montenegrin.

The legend of Montenegro is the *ambiance* of its history. Those who prize the fighter's courage and a nation's
will to freedom recognize that the history of Montenegro,
in the daring and the suffering of its people, generation
after generation, is unequaled in Europe. Serbian by race,
Orthodox by faith, Montenegrin by choice, they were,

from the fifteenth to the nineteenth centuries, the sole people in all the Balkan peninsula who were never wholly subjugated by the Ottoman Turks or, subsequently, by any of the European powers. While the Turks were besieging Vienna in 1529 and again in 1683 and threatening central Europe, there remained at their backs a free Christian principality that, despite the incredibly disproportionate numbers opposite, never failed to withstand them.

The first Montenegrins were Slavic tribes who overran the old Roman province of Illyria during the sixth and seventh centuries; among them were clansmen who settled in the small crater-like valleys lying amidst the barren mountains bounded on the west by the Adriatic Sea and on the east by the Macedonian plain. (From a distance the cold, gray karst ridges of Montenegro actually appear black, hence, presumably, the name "black mountains"—*Crnagora* in Serbian, *Montenegro* in Italian—although the name may possibly be derived from an early ruling family, *Crnojević*.) During the thirteenth and fourteenth centuries Montenegro (then known as Zeta) was ruled by princes of the Nemanja dynasty of Serbia. The Nemanja kings created a great empire which at its zenith, under Tsar Stefan Dušan, stretched from the Hungarian plain to the gates of Constantinople.

In June of 1389, on *Vidov Dan* (the day when "we shall see" what happens), tragedy befell the Serbs and their allies at the Battle of Kosovo. *Vidov Dan* is a date as familiar to every Serb as his own birthday, for it commemorates valor in defeat—the sorest trial of courage—and it gave rise to a magnificent epic poetry woven about the legendary promise that one day the Slavs would again be free and united. After Kosovo many Serbians, still resisting, fled to the rocky fastness of Montenegro and there founded clans which were to become the curse, if also the glory, of that country until modern times. It was these clansmen's fanatical pride in the exclusiveness of their families that led them to measure heroism as a vindication of one's name, thereby encouraging the blood feuds that, oftentimes no less than the constant threat of the Turks, caused Montenegrins until late in the nineteenth century to wear pistols as part of their daily dress.

A second *Vidov Dan* awaited the Montenegrins at the end of the seventeenth century. Following the last of the Crnojević ruling family, the land had been for two centuries governed—to the uncertain extent the clansmen would submit to agreement—by *vladike,* or prince-bishops, who were popularly elected and consecrated by the Serbian Orthodox Patriarch at Peć. But the constant Turkish invasions had made inroads into Montenegro. Cetinje, the capital, had three times been sacked, and mosques appeared in some villages as apostasy spread. In 1697 the clansmen gave to Vladika Danilo Petrović of Njegoši (the Petrović ancestral home) the right to choose his successor from his family, thus establishing a theocratic rule in which, because the bishops were unmarried, succession passed from uncle to nephew. The literary epic poem *Gorski Vijenac,* or "Mountain Wreath," written by the foremost Serbian poet, Njegoš (who was, as Peter II, prince-bishop of Montenegro from 1830 to 1851), describes the terrible decision confronting Vladika Danilo in sending the small Montenegrin force against those of his people who had under duress embraced Islam. The Cross was raised against the Crescent and a frightful slaughter followed. Montenegro was saved, as it had been wrought, in blood.

What the Montenegrins had proclaimed for four centuries, their independence, was at the end of the eighteenth century recognized by the powers of Europe. Under the greatest of the prince-bishops, Peter I, who ruled from 1782 to 1830, the Montenegrins allied themselves with the Russian Tsar and with Serbia, which had in this period finally won its complete independence from the Turks. Led by Peter I and his successor, Peter II (the poet Njegoš), Montenegro carried the struggle relentlessly, year by year, to the Turks on all sides—to Bosnia and Hercegovina on the north and east, to South Serbia and Macedonia on the east, and to Albania on the south. The cost of their freedom was great, not alone because men must pay for it with their lives, but also because men will differ over what freedom is.

III

It is at this period of his homeland's history, in the mid-nineteenth century, that Milovan Djilas begins the account of his family's life in a land without justice, as he calls Montenegro, quoting Njegoš, who despaired often of bringing law and education to his *besudnja zemlja,* which can literally be translated as "land without recourse." Njegoš, indeed, had reason to despair of the Djilas family in the person of Milovan's grandfather's uncle, the outlaw Marko, who flouted the prince-bishop's law against blood feuds. Marko was later murdered by a captain sent by Danilo II, the prince (no longer bishop) who succeeded Peter II and ruled until 1860. Aleksa Djilas, the grandfather of Milovan, avenged Marko's murder and fled to Nikšić, an area inhabited by Montenegrins who were then under Turkish rule. From that time, after 1860, until the founding of Yugoslavia in 1918, the destiny of the Djilas family, as of all Montenegrins, was in the hands of Prince (later King) Nikola, a cunning and capricious but also talented autocrat who was a soldier, historian, and poet. After Aleksa Djilas returned to his home in "Old" Montenegro, at Župa, during the Serbian-Montenegrin war against Turkey in 1875–1878, he was murdered, probably with the cognizance of Prince Nikola. Aleksa was not avenged by his son, Nikola Djilas, but the son, too, was suspected of plots against the Prince and was briefly imprisoned. When he pleaded his loyalty he was freed and later given land, as an officer in the Montenegrin army, at Kolašin, on the border of Turkish territory. There his son Milovan grew to manhood.

Three more wars were to embroil the independent nation of Montenegro during Milovan's lifetime, and in each his father fought, as practically every Montenegrin male in every generation had fought. In 1912, when Milovan was a year old, his father went off to the First Balkan War, and in 1913 he took part in the border skirmishes following the Second Balkan War. In 1914, on June 28, which was *Vidov Dan,* a Serb patriot and conspirator assassinated Archduke Francis Ferdinand of Austria and set off the Great War. That year and the next Djilas's father and uncles fought the encroaching Austrians and Germans, only to be betrayed, in Milovan's view, by King Nikola, who surrendered his armies before they could at least aid the retreating Serbians. He describes the last decisive battle, at Mojkovac, in his novel *Montenegro.*

Milovan Djilas was seven years old when Montenegro was unified, at the end of 1918, with the Serbs and Croats and Slovenes under the Serbian monarch in the kingdom that was later called Yugoslavia. He was eighteen when a Montenegrin delegate killed the Croat leader Radić in the Yugoslav Parliament and thereby hastened the events that led King Alexander to declare a dictatorship. At eighteen, too, he was already a Communist as he went off to Belgrade to study at the University. He was twenty-two, in 1933, when he was imprisoned for three years by the royal government for his Communist activities. At the prison at Sremska Mitrovica he met a fellow prisoner, Alexander Ranković, who years later, as head of the secret police of Communist Yugoslavia, was to order the several arrests of Milovan Djilas that returned him to the same prison cell, only now for a different heresy. In *Land Without Justice* Djilas asks: "Are men doomed to become the slaves of the times in which they live, even when, after irrepressible and tireless effort, they have climbed so high as to become the masters of the times?"

Even were it not for such historical ironies, and its undoubted historical importance, Djilas's autobiography would be a rare book. It is the work of a poet, telling sad brave tales. It could not be otherwise than sad. Extraordinary numbers of Djilas's family, friends, and schoolmates were destroyed by war and revolution. Each had his loyalties, as honest men must, and it was their loyalties that often tore father from son, brother from brother. And who is to tell the right of it, in a land where history makes men choose, if they will not inherit, their faiths? The past echoes in Djilas's words. Kosovo echoes here over a vale of five hundred years when Djilas speaks of the Montenegrin defeat during World War I: "the grandeur of the holocaust at Mojkovac was not in victory, for there was none."

Djilas has the ear and eye of a poet, and juxtaposed with the many oracular statements in his writing will be found colorful and arresting phrases, as when he tells of a Serbian soldier who "spoke in a drawl and softly, like feathers on a wound." There is in Djilas's thoughts, as well, that mixture of precise observation and generalized reflection one finds in Dostoevski. (*The Possessed* might well include a judgment such as Djilas makes in *Land Without Justice:* "Boričić was essentially a good and noble man but an amateur, and deeply unhappy. He had realized nothing of what he had loved and desired.") Djilas's writings do not easily fit into any literary genre. Each moves at its own pace and carries distinctively its own meanings. Yet in the rhythm of his words and in the recurrence of his theme of suffering and joy, death and life, his writing is akin to the epic poetry a Montenegrin sings, alone, to the accompaniment of the almost hypnotically mournful music of his national instrument, the gusle.

A Vision of Good and
Evil:
Part Two

As the case of Milovan Djilas has been reported around
the world, one realizes that the Yugoslavs are as much
puzzled as angered by what they regard as an intrusion by
foreigners into their internal affairs. For them, presumably, Djilas is not important politically. Indeed, I do not
recall a single Yugoslav having said that Djilas has partisan
followers in his country, or that he could, under favorable
circumstance, become an opposition leader to the regime.
Nor do the Yugoslavs wish to take Djilas seriously as a
"personality," taking this term from the peculiar Communist lexicon that makes rather rigid distinctions between policies (abstractions) and people (personality). To
them Djilas is capricious, "not serious," and even as a
writer they should prefer to think him unoriginal.

Given their own view, they cannot quite comprehend
why Djilas appeals so persistently to foreigners, and no

doubt their puzzlement is deepened by the fact that Djilas cannot simply be dismissed as a reactionary and that, in fact, his friends abroad are for the most part liberals, the very people who are generally sympathetic to Yugoslavia itself. (Djilas's book *Conversations with Stalin* is dedicated to Aneurin Bevan who, together with his wife, Jennie Lee, was his most important friend in Great Britain. Further, it has been said that Prime Minister Jawaharlal Nehru interceded with Tito during Djilas's first imprisonment with the result of having him removed from solitary confinement.) Curiously, at least one Yugoslav leader takes Djilas seriously as a "personality"—Marshal Tito himself. Foreign correspondents tell of a press conference in 1954, during which Tito, wishing to put an end to the inevitable questions that would be posed about Djilas's downfall, opened the conference by speaking briefly about the "case." As he spoke Tito became increasingly emotional, until finally he was pounding the table before him with his knuckles, and with the huge ring he wears, to the accompaniment of the declaration "Djido is dead politically! Djido is finished!" That Tito should use the intimate diminutive "Djido" at such a moment suggests that for him Djilas is like a son who has disgraced a still-loving father. Or perhaps Djilas is Tito's "bishop's beggar," as in the Stephen Vincent Benét story in which the bishop is daily reminded, by the presence outside the cathedral of a lame beggar who was in the bishop's youth struck down by his clerical carriage, that a toll is always taken for power.

In the United States the case of Milovan Djilas has been reported regularly but never so intensively as during the occasion of his last arrest, in April of 1962, as a result of the then-forthcoming publication of *Conversations with Stalin*. The transcript of my own testimony before a sub-committee of the United States Senate I give here exactly as it was printed by the subcommittee following the hearing. It hardly needs embellishment, although my journey to Yugoslavia on the hopeless mission to assist Djilas had aspects of melodrama that are not described here. (At one point, as I was about to depart for Belgrade, a United States Senator contemplated issuing a subpoena and ordering a federal marshal to remove me from the airplane on the grounds that I was taking from this country a document—presumably the manuscript of the book—valuable to United States security.) Yet the attention paid by the subcommittee members and their staff to the arrest of Djilas (as well as to the role that Yugoslav officials in the United States played in it) was not only responsible but conducted with a serious respect for a complex situation. My own understanding of the function of Congressional hearings was enhanced by this experience. In any event, the case of Milovan Djilas is not finally or wholly that of interference in the internal

affairs of Yugoslavia, but also that of our concern for a
writer who has been stilled. No one is so richly endowed
with a vision of the ideal that he can afford to ignore
another's.

YUGOSLAV INTERFERENCE WITH
A U.S. BOOK PUBLISHER

Wednesday, June 27, 1962

U.S. SENATE,

SUBCOMMITTEE TO INVESTIGATE THE

ADMINISTRATION OF THE INTERNAL SECURITY ACT

AND OTHER INTERNAL SECURITY LAWS, OF

THE COMMITTEE ON THE JUDICIARY,

Washington, D.C.

The subcommittee met, pursuant to call, at 10:45
a.m., in room 1318, New Senate Office Building,
Senator Olin D. Johnston, presiding.

PRESENT: Senators Johnston, Everett McKinley Dirksen,
and Kenneth B. Keating.

ALSO PRESENT: J. G. Sourwine, chief counsel; Benjamin
Mandel, director of research; and Frank Schroeder,
chief investigator.

SENATOR JOHNSTON. The Subcommittee on Internal Security will come to order.

We have met here this morning on a matter concerning Yugoslav interference with a U.S. publisher. So I will ask counsel to call the first witness.

MR. SOURWINE. Mr. Jovanovich.

SENATOR JOHNSTON. Hold up your right hand. Do you swear the evidence you give before this subcommittee to be the truth, the whole truth, and nothing but the truth, so help you God?

MR. JOVANOVICH. I do, sir.

Testimony of William Jovanovich

MR. SOURWINE. Would you give the reporter your full name and your residence address?

MR. JOVANOVICH. 92 Birch Road, Briarcliff Manor, N.Y.

MR. SOURWINE. What is your business or profession?

MR. JOVANOVICH. I am a book publisher.

MR. SOURWINE. With what company?

MR. JOVANOVICH. I am president of Harcourt, Brace & World in New York City; president of Longmans Canada, Ltd., in Canada, and chairman of Rupert Hart-Davis, London.

MR. SOURWINE. How long have you been in the publishing business, Mr. Jovanovich?

MR. JOVANOVICH. Fifteen years.

MR. SOURWINE. And how long have you held your present position as head of Harcourt, Brace & World?

MR. JOVANOVICH. Seven and a half years.

MR. SOURWINE. Harcourt, Brace & World has recently published a book by Milovan Djilas, is that correct?

MR. JOVANOVICH. Yes sir.

MR. SOURWINE. This was one of several of Djilas' manuscripts which came to you largely because of your friendship, your personal friendship with Mr. Djilas?

MR. JOVANOVICH. Yes, sir.

MR. SOURWINE. Before you published this manuscript, do you recall efforts which were made to interfere with its publication, threats which were made against Mr. Djilas, veiled threats of harm to him in the event the book was published?

MR. JOVANOVICH. Mr. Sourwine, I don't know that I would call them threats. I suppose it always is a matter of definition. You can say it was suggested to me that it would be well for me to withdraw publication of the book in view of the fact that I cared about the fate of Mr. Djilas.

MR. SOURWINE. Mr. Jovanovich, will you, in your own words, tell us about this—give us the background of how you got the Djilas manuscript, and what happened, and go ahead and tell us the story in your own words?

MR. JOVANOVICH. Milovan Djilas, as you know, was one of the four leaders of Yugoslavia following the ascension of the Tito regime in Yugoslavia after World War II. He was, by 1954—when, by his own actions, he fell from power—one of the four chief leaders and was widely considered to be perhaps the heir apparent to Tito himself. He was chairman of the parliament, actually, when he was removed from the Central Committee of the Communist Party.

He fell from power chiefly owing to his criticism of the government and of Communist policy in general, criticism which he, as a Communist official, aired in the press, Borba, the official organ of the Yugoslav Communist Party.

After his fall from power, he became a private citizen. But in 1956 his difficulties with the government began, owing to publication of his articles, first in the New York Times, later in the New Leader. He was sentenced and tried, and given a suspended sentence. And subsequently, when he criticized the action in the Hungarian revolution, he was sentenced again and imprisoned.

MR. SOURWINE. You mean criticized the Soviet action?

MR. JOVANOVICH. Yes, sir. He was imprisoned then in 1957. But before he was imprisoned, he sent out of Yugoslavia two manuscripts. One was the famous book "The New Class" which was published by another American publisher. The second was the first volume of his autobiography, called "Land Without Justice," which I published. "The New Class" created a great stir throughout the world. Djilas was returned to the court and given an additional sentence—although he was then, as I say, in prison—as a result of the publication of "The New Class."

He was in jail 4 years and 2 months, 20 months of which were spent in solitary confinement. Upon his release he was paroled. In January of 1961 he wrote me, either the same day he was released or the day after, and said that he had, in his possession—or would soon receive from the prison officials who would turn back to him his writings—three manuscripts.

I went to Yugoslavia in March of 1961, and at that time spent 5 days with Milovan Djilas, discussing his manuscripts. These were first, a novel laid in World War I, called "Montenegro." Second, a biography of the greatest Serbo-Croatian writer, Njegoš. Third, a collection of tales, or short stories.

It was at this time that Djilas told me that he intended to write a fourth book about his experiences on missions to Moscow and meetings with Stalin, and he intended to write it during that summer, which he subsequently did.

In December of 1961, through the mail, I received from Djilas the manuscript for the novel, the manuscript for the biography of Njegoš, and the book "Conversations with Stalin."

The decision on my part to publish "Conversations" as the first of these books was not, curiously enough, related to anything having to do with the book as such. The biography of Njegoš is an extremely long, scholarly, and very complicated work. I am still struggling in the translation and editing. I am not doing the translation myself. But it will require still another year's work. The novel required some editing. But the "Conversations with Stalin" was so direct, so beautifully organized and written in so simple a style, that it was possible to translate it rapidly, and schedule publication as I did for May of this year.

I went back to Yugoslavia in March 1962—late February and early March 1962—to see Djilas again. And at that time I carried the proofs of the book "Conversations with Stalin." He and I spent time revising it. He added sections which I then translated, and we went over various parts of it together.

While I was there, the first hint of trouble—I shouldn't say the first hint, let us say the first overt action on the part of the Yugoslav Government— which suggested that publication would bring trouble, took place. I believe it was on March 2 or 3. I actually was in Djilas' apartment when one of his friends came with a copy of Borba, the official Communist newspaper, attacking a magazine called Tempo Presente, which is edited by the famous Italian writer and ex-Communist, Ignacio Silone. In

this magazine was a story, one of the tales in this
collection I mentioned earlier, which Djilas had sent
to Silone. It is a story called "War." The story had
no mention of Yugoslavia or of the national libera-
tion army—that is the partisan army. It had no
mention of anything in a direct sense political to
Yugoslavia. But it was a condemnation of the brutality of people in war and the tragedy of people in
war. The Yugoslav Government had banned this
magazine. I would guess not more than 50 copies are
sent into Yugoslavia normally. But they banned this
magazine. They made no mention of the reason—
they made mention of the reason that it had this
story "War" in it, but they made no mention of
Djilas as the author of the story.

It was at this time that I told Djilas of my very great
fears that publication of "Conversations with Stalin"
would create an extremely difficult situation for him.
But he didn't feel that this would occur, or if he did
feel that it would occur, at any rate he didn't dissent,
and he urged me to go ahead with publication.

(*Senator Keating enters the hearing room.*)

MR. JOVANOVICH. I left Yugoslavia—I believe the date was
March 4, 1962. Up to this point I had not announced
the existence of this book, except, curiously enough,
in Yugoslavia. I had, when I arrived at the end of
February, said to Djilas that I thought that it might

be well, since I had all along treated this book not as a sensational document, nor as something that was propaganda—a propaganda instrument—that it might be well for me in my dealings with other Yugoslav publishers and writers to mention the existence of this book in a calm and regular way, as one of several publications. I had on my list several other Yugoslav books. Djilas agreed to this, and so I did mention it to some Yugoslavs during that visit of early March 1962.

MR. SOURWINE. Did you mention it to anyone connected with the Government?

MR. JOVANOVICH. I mentioned it to publishers and editors.

(*Senator Dirksen enters the hearing room.*)

MR. JOVANOVICH. Now, whether any of them was connected with the Government, Mr. Sourwine, I wouldn't know. This was done with Djilas' cognizance. That was the first mention, as I say.

Before I left March 4 to go to Paris, Djilas and I agreed that, since I had not publicized the existence of this book, perhaps the most sensible way to announce its existence would be to let one newspaper, one columnist, if you will, speak of the book. And so, when I got to Paris, I showed the galleys to C. L. Sulzberger of the New York Times. He returned the galleys to me. And subsequently, on April 2, he published a column about the existence of the book, quoting from it.

This was not, however, the first mention of the book in this way in the American press.

Unbeknownst to me, that is unbeknownst to me until mid-April, Djilas had, I believe the very day I left, March 4, or perhaps the next day, told the story of the book to a woman named Desa Bourne, who is correspondent for the London Times. She is a Yugoslav by birth, and now a British subject, married to a man named Eric Bourne, who is the correspondent for the Christian Science Monitor. Djilas had at great length described the book to her, allowed her to look at the manuscript, and she apparently took copious notes. She then turned over these notes to her husband, Mr. Bourne. And as a result—I am not sure of my dates, Mr. Sourwine, on this—on March 30 or 31, I think, the Christian Science Monitor ran an article under Eric Bourne's byline about the book. So that my attempts to give Sulzberger the first notice of the book turned out by accident not to be the first, but the second.

I had scheduled publication of the book for mid-May. Sulzberger's piece came out April 2. Beginning April 3, an attaché in the New York consulate, named Drago Vujica—

MR. SOURWINE. That is the New York consulate of Yugoslavia.

MR. JOVANOVICH. The New York consulate of Yugoslavia. He attempted to get in touch with me. And through a series of mishaps, owing to my being away from town, and one thing or another, I didn't actually see him—I didn't actually talk to him—until April 5. At that time he said it was a matter of great urgency, and asked to see me. I agreed to stop by the consulate on Fifth Avenue on my way down to my office, on the morning of Friday, April 6. I then went to see Mr. Vujica, whom I had met and had known previously. Mr. Vujica said he had had word from Belgrade that the forthcoming publication of the book was a matter of grave and urgent concern to the Yugoslavs, and that the Yugoslavs considered the book to be harmful to Yugoslav interests. Mr. Vujica's attitude was that as a friend to Yugoslavia, as a second generation American of Yugoslav descent, surely I didn't want to do anything that was harmful to Yugoslav interests, that was egregious, or superficially harmful for no purpose at all. I then denied that the book was harmful to Yugoslav interests, and said to Mr. Vujica, that indeed the Yugoslavs emerged from the book as being quite heroic and brave in the face of Soviet imprecations during the 1948 crisis, when Yugoslavia broke with the Soviet Union. This discussion went on for a bit. And finally Mr. Vujica said, "Well of course your opinion that it is not harmful is one we can't corroborate, because we haven't seen the book."

Later he said that, since I was a friend of Djilas, I wouldn't want any harm to come to Djilas either; would I? And I said, "No."

So then I said, "Well, Mr. Vujica, I don't feel we are getting anywhere in this discussion. I think the book is not harmful, and I don't see how it could be harmful to Mr. Djilas either. But you say you haven't read it, and consequently this is an uneven discussion. I will send you two proof copies of the book, and I would suggest that you and the Consul General let me know in about 10 days what your opinion of it is."

All through this discussion Mr. Vujica said he thought the best thing would be for me to withdraw the book. I did not at that time agree either to withdraw the book or to postpone it during this conversation. However, I left the consulate and went back to my office, and felt that this was indeed a most serious situation for Djilas.

MR. SOURWINE. You got the definite impression that there had been an attempt to convey to you, a successful attempt to convey to you, that there was danger for Djilas if the book became published.

MR. JOVANOVICH. Yes; I think that was the impression, Mr. Sourwine.

When I got back to the office, I was in a rather depressed mood about this, and decided that it would be well to postpone publication of the book. I had announced publication, I believe, on April 5, perhaps April 4, to the press; that is, the formal announcement, that it was to be published on such and such a day. And so I did, on April 6, when I got back to the office, tell our publicity department to send out a notice to all newspapers and reviewers, and so forth, that the book had been postponed—no explanation. I then sent to Mr. Vujica two proof copies of the book with a note saying that I had postponed publication for a short time, and that I would expect to hear from him and the Consul General by April 17, roughly 10 days.

MR. SOURWINE. Did you meanwhile call in any outstanding proof copies of the book?

MR. JOVANOVICH. I believe there were—I am not sure of this, Mr. Sourwine, I don't have my records—but I guess there were seven or eight out in the hands of people like Time magazine and others. I called back proof copies. I called back proof copies from some private readers. I believe I had sent a proof copy to Walter Lippmann and McGeorge Bundy, and I asked for those back.

Then the next morning I learned that Djilas had been re-arrested in Belgrade. I called Vujica, who said he didn't know about this, and I said that I would like to obtain a visa to go to Yugoslavia. I didn't at that time say why I wanted to go to Yugoslavia. I simply said I wanted to go. I did apply for a visa. And on my visa I said I wanted to see authors and publishers, which is what I always put on the visa, and which was indeed true.

On April 9 I came to Washington for a number of purposes, one in part to see an architect who is consulting on the construction of our new building. And also in part to see the State Department.

On April 10, Vujica called me—

MR. SOURWINE. Pardon me, sir. Whom did you see in the State Department?

MR. JOVANOVICH. Mr. Mudd at the Southern European Section.

MR. SOURWINE. What was the purpose of that trip?

MR. JOVANOVICH. What was my purpose, sir?

MR. SOURWINE. Yes, sir.

MR. JOVANOVICH. My purpose, I think, was threefold. First, I wanted to make it known that I was going. Secondly, I wanted to obtain an interview, if possible, with Ambassador Kennan. I thought the proper way to do that would be to tell the State Department beforehand. And thirdly, I thought it would be well for the State Department to know what the general background and situation was.

Mr. Vujica called me while I was in Washington, April 10, and said that I had been granted my visa.

MR. SOURWINE. Where did he reach you?

MR. JOVANOVICH. Well, through a mixup, he didn't reach me at the hotel. He reached me at the State Department. The phone company, I think, was overzealous, or overefficient. The call got switched over to the State Department, although I had asked for it to be kept at the hotel. And I was in the State Department at the time. He said I had my visa, and he said "You will not get your—you will not hear from us in New York." He was obviously referring to my note, in which I had said that I would like to hear by April 17 from the Consul General himself on whether or not the publication of the book was harmful and by implication to Djilas.

MR. SOURWINE. Did you ask him if that is what he meant?

MR. JOVANOVICH. I didn't press it. He just said twice "You will not hear from us in New York." I took this to mean that I might indeed hear in Belgrade. I took it as an encouraging sign that I might be able to talk with the people in Belgrade about this matter. Now, whether I read into what he said more than he intended, I cannot say.

I left New York, flying to Zurich, that evening.
When I got to Zurich, I was met by a British news-
paperman and said that my purpose was, if possible,
to see Mr. Djilas and to find out what his situation
was. I arrived in Belgrade that evening, met by the
entire press corps in Belgrade, which had gathered
there—most of them are stationed in Vienna—as Gromyko was coming on April 16, the following Mon-
day. And so they had gathered to prepare for this
occasion.

I then held a press conference, substantially saying
that my purpose was, if possible, to see Mr. Djilas,
and to do what I could in his interest.

I did not at any point say that I would withdraw the
publication of the book. Now, I don't want to be
disingenuous about this. The press took up the implication that I was willing to withdraw the book if
Djilas would be released, and I did nothing to correct
that implication. But I would like to point out
formally, officially, literally, I never did make the
offer.

Subsequently, while I was in Belgrade, I tried to see
Djilas. I went to the Bureau of Internal Affairs. There
I had, as has been quoted in the press, an almost
Kafka-like experience of being told that one couldn't
apply to see a man who was free. And as I say, there
was a sort of frightening logic about this, because as

the Yugoslav press and radio had not announced his arrest, he was, in the view of Yugoslav citizens, indeed free. The rest of the world knew he wasn't, but apparently the Yugoslavs didn't.

I then finally, through many moves, did obtain an interview with Enver Humo, who is the Secretary of Information, and during this conversation with Mr. Humo, I was told by him that my visit really was quite fruitless, that I had made a contract with a known convict and that circumstances that had ensued should not surprise me, for Mr. Djilas' criminality had been already established by the newspaper accounts of the forthcoming publication of the book. I was told also by Mr. Humo that my opinions on whether or not the book was harmful to Yugoslavia were irrelevant, I was a foreign subject—he told me that I was a foreign subject at least 16 times, as if this were a startling piece of information. And he said there was no question as to the fact of his guilt. The newspaper accounts of the book were sufficient to establish his guilt. Now, I don't mean to imply that he said at any point that it didn't make any difference whether the book was published or not. He didn't say that. He simply said there was no—in effect he said there was nothing I could do, there was no one I could talk with, there were no propositions I could put forth that would bear on the case.

Subsequently, I did, through a third person, write to Crnobrnja, who is the Secretary General to Marshal Tito, and received a reply, again through this third person, that there was not any point in further discussion. According to Crnobrnja, I had had my responsible reply from the Yugoslav Government.

I then left Yugoslavia on the morning of April 16, which, again, was the day Gromyko was arriving.

On the plane coming back, I was faced with the decision whether or not to publish the book. I had not seen Djilas. I had seen his wife every day during my visit, and for many, many hours. She left the decision entirely in my hands. I then decided, and, on my arrival in New York, announced that I would publish the book on May 25. This turned out to be a sort of lunatic accident. I had simply chosen a date 8 days later than the original publication date, assuming that the whole process of publishing had been delayed that long, and I happened to have chosen Tito's birthday. Subsequently, I got letters from European correspondents saying what a misfortune this was. But I didn't change the date.

MR. SOURWINE. Why was it a misfortune to publish Djilas' book on Tito's birthday?

MR. JOVANOVICH. Well, Borba—the official newspaper— finally announced Djilas' arrest. And in this article announcing his arrest, dwelled at great length on my own role in this, saying that at first I had been disingenuous, I had said that the book was of historical interest, a memoir. Later I became more honest—I think these were the words of Borba—and admitted that this was a propaganda instrument—I don't know where they got this "admission." And that finally the extent of my deviousness was revealed by the fact that I had chosen the very date of the Marshal's 70th birthday to publish the book.

You will understand, Mr. Sourwine, that there is an extraordinary sensitivity among the Yugoslavs on things that perhaps wouldn't bother you or me, but indeed do bother them.

Well, I did publish the book on May 25. I have had no further relations with anybody in Yugoslavia. I have written to Mrs. Djilas on three occasions. I have received no reply.

The only other thing that has happened that relates to the Yugoslavs is that I wrote the Consul General in New York about a week ago, saying that, in the court sentence that was passed on Djilas' trial, it was said that the court would confiscate any royalties from "Conversations with Stalin." And I wrote to the Consul General saying I was aware of this judgment, but that I had royalties from "Land Without Justice," the earlier book I had published in 1958, and had he any suggestions as to how I could send such moneys to Mrs. Djilas without causing difficulty or confusion. I have received no reply.

Djilas was tried in a secret trial, a closed trial. He was condemned to 8 years, 8 months, imprisonment, 3 years and 8 months of which are the continuation of the former term—that is the revocation of his parole —and five years of which are a sentence based on a law passed March 17, which is an interesting date. The existence of the book was then known. And this law says that any Yugoslav who, as an official or former official of Yugoslavia, publishes information he obtained as an official that was or could be harmful to the Yugoslav state, was liable to imprisonment and 10 years hard labor.

MR. SOURWINE. Then Mr. Djilas was convicted and sentenced to three and a half years of hard labor under a law that was passed after the alleged offense was committed.

MR. JOVANOVICH. Yes, sir, it is a retroactive law. The existence of the book was known. It is also a rather interesting law, because I think if one carried it to its logical extent, there are quite a few Yugoslav officials, or ex-officials, perhaps even the Marshal himself, who have revealed information which in a later context might be considered harmful to the Yugoslav interests. But it is not for me to judge what they had in mind in their jurisdictional procedure.

I say they were aware of the book because it was mailed in December of 1961. Let's assume that the manuscript came through the mail without examination. Still, I did mention the existence of the book to several Yugoslavs March 1, 2, 3. Djilas himself was interrogated about the book, and—I am sorry I don't have my notes on this—I think he was asked to submit the manuscript to the Department of Justice of Serbia. He was interrogated on April 2 by one of the prosecutors or inspectors, or justices—I haven't got the exact terminology—on April 2, about the book. He was arrested on April 7.

Well, that, sir, is, briefly stated, or perhaps not so briefly stated, the background.

MR. SOURWINE. Have you had any word from Mr. Djilas since his arrest and incarceration?

MR. JOVANOVICH. No, sir. I heard from a correspondent that he was alive and well. He is in the central prison apparently in Belgrade. The reason he apparently has not been moved to Sremska Mitrovica, which is the Serbian state prison, where he had spent his previous 4 years and 2 months—and where ironically he had also been imprisoned 3 years—1933 to 1936—as a Communist, by the royal Yugoslav Government—is because his wife entered an appeal. Now, as I understand it, the appeal really is against the jurisdictional procedure rather than against the sentence as such.

Presumably, if the appeal is turned down, he will then be moved to Sremska Mitrovica, to serve out his term.

This correspondent also told me that he was denied writing materials, and was writing on toilet paper.

MR. SOURWINE. He is still writing?

MR. JOVANOVICH. He is still writing. He will always go on writing.

MR. SOURWINE. Do you plan to go ahead and publish the other books by Djilas, of which you have manuscripts?

MR. JOVANOVICH. Yes, sir; I intend to publish the novel next spring, possibly the short stories the following fall, that is the fall of 1963, and the biography of Njegoš, the spring or fall of 1964.

MR. SOURWINE. Have you had any other experiences during your publishing experience in efforts of a foreign government to interfere with the publication of a book in the United States?

MR. JOVANOVICH. No sir. I have published other Yugoslav books, and have very good relations indeed with the Yugoslav publishers. And during the past 2 years I have advised Yugoslav publishers, and indeed tried to help Yugoslav writers as well as I could in my capacity.

I am not so sure that "interference" is the right word. You know, it is really quite possible that you could come to me and say "I don't think the publication of a book would be well. It might hurt these people—some person." I have known of instances like this. This might be construed by me to be an opinion on your part. I don't know that I would consider it strict interference.

MR. SOURWINE. Well, I don't know why you used me for an example. But taking me as an example, I would have no power over Milovan Djilas, would I, to do him harm?

MR. JOVANOVICH. Sir?

MR. SOURWINE. I would have no power over Milovan Djilas to do him harm?

MR. JOVANOVICH. No, that is true.

MR. SOURWINE. Whereas the Yugoslav Government had that power, and the impression was, at least you understood, that that power would be used if the book was published, and that Djilas might be harmed.

MR. JOVANOVICH. That is true. I would agree fully with that. What I am saying though—

MR. SOURWINE. That is nothing more nor less than blackmail, is it?

MR. JOVANOVICH. Well, I suppose—yes, if it is more firmly put. But I was never told, you see, that he would not be harmed if I withdrew the book. Let's say that it was very subtle blackmail at the best.

174

MR. SOURWINE. The touch was light.

MR. JOVANOVICH. The touch was extremely light, yes. What I was trying to say, Mr. Sourwine—I think we are talking about the same thing—but I was under no compunction to agree. I was under no—in short, I had perfect free will in the situation. So that while they did hold over me something that was indeed dreadful to me, which was harm to Mr. Djilas, I don't think they were under any illusions that I couldn't go ahead as I wished.

SENATOR JOHNSTON. When did you first find out about this law that they put into existence in March?

MR. JOVANOVICH. Curiously enough, Senator, I didn't know about that law immediately. It was enacted on March 17. I only learned about the full extent of the law by translation from a Swiss newspaper about April 4, and I immediately wrote Djilas a long letter, which presumably arrived the day after he was arrested, and was never received. And I wrote him at great length in this letter that I had just discovered the full text of this law, and that I was gravely concerned.

SENATOR JOHNSTON. Did he at any time tell you that he knew of this law being in existence?

MR. JOVANOVICH. No, sir. You see, I left March 4. The law was passed March 17. And I had no correspondence— rather, I had correspondence from him, but there was no mention of this law.

SENATOR JOHNSTON. But you know he is serving at the present time because he did give you the right to publish this book.

MR. JOVANOVICH. I don't think there is any question that the publication of the book, or, let us say, the forthcoming publication of the book, the handing over of the manuscript, and the subsequent press accounts based on it, were the cause of his trial or revocation of his parole, and the new sentence. There is no question about that.

SENATOR KEATING. Would you be guilty under the same law as a conspirator with him?

MR. JOVANOVICH. I don't see how. I am not an official or an ex-official of Yugoslavia.

SENATOR KEATING. The Yugoslav code doesn't deal with conspiracy? They don't recognize a conspiracy, the way we would in this country.

MR. JOVANOVICH. As an American citizen, I don't see how they would have any jurisdiction.

SENATOR KEATING. I know, not unless you were there.

SENATOR JOHNSTON. I believe, though, you state the law sets forth that you must have been an official of that government.

MR. JOVANOVICH. Or an ex-official.

SENATOR KEATING. Yes. But in this country, a person who conspired with an official to breach the law could be, under our system of justice—

MR. JOVANOVICH. It is an interesting point, Senator. I am not so sure that it is true. Let's say that Senator Nixon, or rather Vice President Nixon, whose book "Six Decisions"—let's say there were an American law of this nature, and he was considered as an ex-official. Incidentally, it was mentioned to me by Mr. Vujica, as an example, that Winston Churchill had asked Parliament, or had asked the Home Secretary, whether or not he could use materials in his history of World War II which he had gleaned as Prime Minister of England. And Vujica cited this as an example that even in the Western Democracies an official had sought approval before he used official information. This was Vujica's statement.

But to get back to the other point, let us say we had such a law in this country, and Vice President Nixon ignored it. I am not at all sure that the publisher would be in any way liable. Under the Bill of Rights he would certainly have very good recourse not to be liable.

SENATOR JOHNSTON. Now, aren't you getting into a field where the wording of the statute would determine the issue?

MR. JOVANOVICH. Well, perhaps I am, Senator. Perhaps it is because I feel very keenly about book publishing being the freest form of expression in America.

SENATOR KEATING. While we recognize the Bill of Rights, I don't imagine the Yugoslavs have a Bill of Rights, at least similar to ours.

MR. JOVANOVICH. Well, of course there is always a question of whether you have laws—and whether you abide by them, too, I suppose.

MR. SOURWINE. Mr. Jovanovich, so the record might read clearly on that, I would like to express a legal opinion off the cuff, which is always dangerous. I think that such a law, if enacted in the United States, would be unconstitutional, both as regards Vice President Nixon and any other author, and as regards you or any other publisher. It wouldn't be a case of the law catching the author and not catching the publisher. The freedom of the press would protect both.

MR. JOVANOVICH. Yes, I think this is a highly academic discussion, and probably fruitless. But I was perhaps trying to glorify the fact that in book publishing there are practically no pressures of any kind in this country. It is to my mind the freest form of expression.

There are not even any advertisers, Mr. Sourwine.

MR. SOURWINE. I have no further questions.

SENATOR KEATING. I have a couple of questions. You have known Djilas for a long time?

MR. JOVANOVICH. Not a long time. I met him only on the two occasions, March of 1961 and March of 1962.

Of course, I have known of him a long time, and we had correspondence. I wrote the introduction to his book "Land Without Justice." When he was released from prison, he wrote me that he felt I understood very well the Montenegrin background. My father was a Montenegrin. But we did on those two occasions spend 5 days with each other in almost constant conversation.

SENATOR KEATING. What was his first offense that he was charged with, for which he served a sentence?

MR. JOVANOVICH. The first offense I think was—and again I don't have the exact record—the first offense I believe was a criticism of Communist philosophy, the Communist doctrine, published in the New York Times. That is the one for which he got a suspended sentence. He was tried, but given a suspended sentence. The second was the criticism of the Soviet action in Hungary, which he characterized as the beginning of the end of communism, and for that he was tried again, and this time sentenced, I think, to 3 years. The third trial had to do with the publication of "The New Class," when he was returned from prison, tried again, and given, I believe, 6 more years.

SENATOR KEATING. When was the trial at which he was convicted for criticizing the Soviet action in Hungary?

MR. JOVANOVICH. I think January 1957, or late 1956—I am
not sure.

SENATOR KEATING. Did you ever discuss with Djilas the
image of Yugoslavia that was being promoted, as
being separate from the Communist bloc, so-called—
the Communist bloc countries?

MR. JOVANOVICH. I discussed at great length with Djilas
the future of communism. Our discussions generally
didn't take the form of any discussion of the Yugoslav
foreign policy in relation to the West and the East,
but rather discussions about the Soviet Union, Communist philosophy, and Communist practice, the
weaknesses in the Communist system, and so forth.
I don't recall that he ever specifically spoke of the
situation of Yugoslavia in either the Eastern or
Western blocs, or as a neutralist nation.

SENATOR KEATING. You didn't discuss that particularly?

MR. JOVANOVICH. Well, particularly I think, Senator, for
the reason that Djilas is a poet, and a philosopher,
and he is deeply interested in the nature of communism. I don't mean he is not also interested in the
practical political effects of international relations.
But as sometimes will happen, we discussed this at
such great length we never got around to talking
about the other.

SENATOR KEATING. What is his political orientation—if you
could describe it in terms we would recognize here.

MR. JOVANOVICH. Well, I would say that were he to be identified in the sense of a political organization, his thinking now is fairly close to that of the Social Democrats in Germany, or the Labor Party in Britain, the Christian Democrats in Austria.

SENATOR KEATING. Was he at any time a Communist?

MR. JOVANOVICH. Oh, yes.

SENATOR KEATING. He embraced that philosophy at one time?

MR. JOVANOVICH. He not only embraced it, he helped define it. He was the theoretician of the Yugoslav Communist Party, along with Moshe Pijade. He was, for example, the man who defended the so-called independent communism in Yugoslavia in the 1948 break with the Soviet Union. It was his articles in the press in Yugoslavia which gave to the Yugoslav people, as it were, the philosophical line about independent communism, communism existing independent of the Soviet Union. He was a Communist actually from 1933 to 1954. He suffered greatly as a Communist because he was tortured and imprisoned by the Royal Yugoslav Government from 1933 to 1936. He is not now a Communist, obviously. But I think, as I tried to explain briefly—at a previous occasion—with Djilas it is not defection, and it is not heresy. I think this point means more to me than it does to others, because I don't always get a warm

response when I talk about this. But there isn't in him
any sense of having renounced the religion or having
joined a new one. He is not fanatical in his renunci-
ation. He feels communism went through a phase,
he feels it is fairly well showing signs of decline, he
feels he went through a phase. But, unlike so many
ex-Communists we have discovered in the United
States, he doesn't become another kind of fanatic.

SENATOR KEATING. Were the only American officials who
discussed this book with you—the publication of it—
the men you saw in the State Department on that
occasion when you were called in?

MR. JOVANOVICH. There was just Mr. Mudd.

SENATOR KEATING. Is Djilas now in solitary confinement?

MR. JOVANOVICH. I would presume so. Yes sir.

SENATOR KEATING. There was a time, I believe you indicated in executive session, that his release from
solitary confinement came about as a result of efforts
made by Mr. Nehru in his behalf.

MR. JOVANOVICH. This is what I have been told on very
good authority—that he had been in solitary confinement, I think for a period of 20 months, in an
unheated cell, and—

SENATOR KEATING. In an unheated cell?

MR. JOVANOVICH. This is what I was told. And that Prime
Minister Nehru, in a conversation with Marshal Tito,
suggested that this was inhumane, and he was then

removed from solitary confinement. But whether or not Nehru had anything to do with his subsequent parole or not I have no information. But I do have what I consider very reliable information that Nehru did effect the bettering of his prison conditions.

SENATOR KEATING. Is there any action which you think any official of our Government, or the Indian Government, or any other could now take to better his plight in any way, or would any such action do him more harm than good?

MR. JOVANOVICH. Well, Senator, I don't think he can be done very much more harm than he has been done, short of being killed. I don't think the American press, the American Congress, and the American executive branch were very active or helpful during his previous imprisonment, whereas the British Labor Party was extremely helpful. Aneurin Bevan, to whom he dedicated the book "Conversations with Stalin," was very active in his behalf, as was Jennie Lee, a Member of Parliament, and Aneurin Bevan's wife.

The Socialist Parties, that is the Social Democrats, or the Christian Socialists, were also active in his behalf during his previous imprisonment.

I would think now that there will be, among the Members of Parliament in Britain, particularly among the Labor Party—I don't know why I say that, for I see no reason why not also among the Conservatives—some efforts being made. I should think among the Italian Party some efforts are being made, and among the German and Austrian. Whether the neutralists, so-called neutralists or non-committed people, such as the Indians, will be of any assistance, I don't know.

On the whole, I don't look for much help for Mr. Djilas from the Americans, because we seem to be in a peculiar position of having to deal always with foreign aid, and I suppose anything that is done officially is construed as a form of blackmail—"we won't give you aid unless you act in a certain way." But I think it is a great pity, because I don't think the American Congress or the American executive or the American press need regard Djilas as a political figure. He is not the head of a political party, he has no followers in Yugoslavia, he is not fomenting any internal revolutions. He is a poet, a philosopher, a writer, a man who has thought deeply about communism, and intends to go on writing. He is in this sense like Boris Pasternak. I think he is an extraordinary writer. He has been a poet always. He has never stopped writing. And his writing gets better and better as he gets freer and freer from Marxist dialectic. But it seems to me that in this country we are perhaps oversensitive to the fact that we might be criticized for saying something of this kind. I don't see any reason why the American Congress or the American executive shouldn't make a strong statement to the effect that this is persecution of a thinking, writing man, and that this is everybody's concern. It isn't an internal affair. I don't think a writer jailed is ever an internal affair. I think it is a world affair.

SENATOR JOHNSTON. Isn't a great deal of the reason that the public has not taken a hand in this the fact that they do not know and have the information that you have?

MR. JOVANOVICH. Well, that may indeed be so, Senator. The book is in existence, his history is known. I don't know how to get this information available to people. It does seem to me of extreme importance that Djilas be kept alive, that he be allowed to write. And I can't help but feel that if the British and the Germans and the Austrians and the Italians, privately or in parties, can bring pressure to bear and bring opinion to bear, as they did in the previous imprisonment, I don't see any reason why the Americans can't as well.

MR. SOURWINE. Your point about aid was an interesting one. Do I understand correctly that what you meant is that the United States, once having undertaken to give foreign aid to a country, is, during the period of such aid, more or less stopped from bringing any pressures on the country for moral purposes or otherwise, for fear that we would be accused of black-mailing the country?

MR. JOVANOVICH. Well, I think, Mr. Sourwine, we have been faced with this the last 15 years. When you help somebody out, they are extremely sensitive to your commenting about their appearance, or anything else, aren't they? I think we are always in that situation. I think the Yugoslavs have become masters at the game of hurt pride, of sensitivity. They are a sensitive, proud people. I am of Yugoslav ancestry, and I am proud of them. But I also think perhaps you can wear pride on your sleeve perhaps a little too much.

SENATOR JOHNSTON. In other words, it is your attitude, then, that we should not make any exceptions, and give to the Communist countries like we give to other countries—is this your attitude?

MR. JOVANOVICH. I am not speaking on the subject of whether foreign aid to a Communist country is desirable or not. I am saying that, on a question of moral integrity, on a question of free speech, I don't see that our position of giving aid is really relevant. I don't see why we can't take a position with a country we give aid to, as well as to a country we don't give aid to. By we, I don't mean the official position, but I mean as Americans of standing, such

as Members of Congress, such as important writers
and the press.

In short, I think that what I am trying to say—perhaps
this is oversimplified—is that, if Djilas were a French-
man and had been treated in this way, I wouldn't
expect that anybody in our Government or in our
press would hesitate to criticize the French Government for what they thought was morally a reprehensible action. Why should we hesitate to criticize
a Communist country to whom we give aid?

SENATOR KEATING. I couldn't agree with you more. I think
you are absolutely right.

MR. JOVANOVICH. I am not suggesting that aid is not desirable. That is not my point.

SENATOR KEATING. You are not getting into the question of
whether or not aid is desirable. What you are saying
is that whether we are giving aid or not giving aid
to a country, if they do something that offends our
sense of inherent justice, there is no harm in our
speaking out about it. I think we should. I agree
with you thoroughly that when a great literary figure
like this is locked up on a political crime in any
country, it is a matter of international concern.

MR. JOVANOVICH. I think so, too, Senator.

SENATOR JOHNSTON. I think we will all agree with you on
that point, as far as that is concerned.

MR. SOURWINE. Mr. Jovanovich, if there were a law enacted in the United States making it an offense to interfere or attempt to interfere with the publication of any book, would it be a protection of material value to the publishing industry?

MR. JOVANOVICH. No, sir. I think what has happened in this case is a very rare instance. If I may say so, Mr. Sourwine, without seeming presumptuous, I hope the Congress doesn't pass any laws about publishing, even to help it. Book publishing in this country is absolutely free.

SENATOR JOHNSTON. In other words, our form of government, under the Constitution, gives you that right, without any laws.

MR. JOVANOVICH. Yes, sir; and it operates magnificently. The Congress perhaps has other more urgent matters, and this is working just fine.

SENATOR KEATING. I suggest, Mr. Chairman, I think all of us—I am sure all of us have deep feeling about the incarceration of Djilas. I would suggest that a copy of this transcript be forwarded to the President and the Secretary of State for review. I don't know myself what we can properly do. I think their attention ought to be called to it at least.

SENATOR JOHNSTON. If there is no objection, it will be referred to them for their consideration, so they will have this before them, for their information.

SENATOR KEATING. Particularly if this man is suffering under solitary confinement as he did for what was it—

MR. JOVANOVICH. Twenty months.

SENATOR KEATING. In an unheated cell—I think all our officials ought to know that. I am not sure just what they can do.

MR. JOVANOVICH. But I think the denial to him, if it is true—and again this is a secondhand report—of writing materials, and reading materials, to him is perhaps even more important.

SENATOR KEATING. About the most cruel punishment you can mete out to him.

MR. JOVANOVICH. Yes, it is.

SENATOR JOHNSTON. Any other questions? The committee will be adjourned subject to the call of the Chair. And we certainly thank you for coming before us and giving us this information. It will be referred to the President and to the State Department.

(*Whereupon, at 11:30 a.m., the committee adjourned, subject to the call of the Chair.*)

Publishing as
a National
Experience

That books should be freely published is the belief of all right-thinking men. Yet it is, I think, a belief that derives in large part from the struggles of newspapers against the intervention of governments, and less from any historical experiences in the publishing of books explicitly. The rights of the "free press" call to mind immediately the rights of newspapers or, on further reflection, of the journals and pamphlets that two and three centuries ago preceded newspapers. American school children are taught the example of John Peter Zenger, the publisher of the New York *Weekly Journal,* whose paper was suppressed in 1734 by the British Governor of New York on the grounds that Zenger had committed criminal libel and who was successfully defended by Andrew Hamilton (who was probably the model for the familiar American idiom "a Philadelphia lawyer"). No American textbook that I know of mentions a book publisher in connection with the First Amendment to the Constitution, guaranteeing the rights of free expression. In recent times, except for the occasional official sorties against books that are charged with pornography, the issue of uncensored publishing is likely to be related to newspapers, as in the Vassal (1962) and Profumo (1963) cases in Great Britain. In this sense, from the view of the book publisher, no news is good news.

There seem to be no major questions about the rights of book publishing in the democratic societies of the West—and there would be fewer minor ones if we could once agree what comprises a lewd or lascivious intent on the part of the contemporary novelist. Indeed, for us it is something of a surprise to realize that a Soviet Premier can be so consciously implicated in his government's vacillating policies, now and again permissive and restrictive, on the publishing of books, as in the instance of Boris Pasternak, and, more recently, Yevgeny Yevtushenko. Possibly this seems unusual because we in the West tend to make a somewhat superficial distinction between the daily press and books vis-à-vis the state, regarding the former as a matter of politics and the latter as a form of culture. The Soviet government, which intrudes a consistent philosophy into both politics and culture, is understandably more aware than Western governments that, as Alfred North Whitehead said, the existing order is always in danger from a general idea. In large part the distinction between newspapers and books, at least as I have posed it here, is owed to a concept of immediacy. Newspapers report and comment on events as they occur, at the moment when partisan passions may be strong or when public policy is uncertain; as a result, their power to shape opinion and even to move governments is appreciated, if also grossly exaggerated. Books are neither written nor published with dispatch, and both authors and publishers are aware, if, to be sure, they aim for excellence, that when a book attempts to report current events it somehow betrays its function and cheapens its presence. In this sense, books are always *after the fact*. Typically, Zenger wrote a book, *A Brief Narrative of the Case and Tryal of John Peter Zenger* (1736), once the immediate issue was resolved.

Even granting that a quality of *laissez faire* prevails in publishing, there are particular questions that need to be raised about present-day book publishing as it relates to government. These are questions publishers *ought* to raise, but I am not hopeful, for too many of them assume that because books are intrinsic to civilized society the traditional course of publishing is assured—that is, if they think on the matter at all. Publishers are not given to reflecting on their profession as a part of the national experience, nor for making a serious connection between books past, books present, and books future. (Harold Macmillan has never made, so far as I know, a statement about his own calling as a publisher that suggested its pertinence to the national interest.) In support of this somewhat self-conscious and aggrieved sentiment, there is the fact that little has been said about the increasing need to define the government's position in determining the content and production of textbooks: this at a time when education has become a dominant public issue, and when the possibility grows that as military expenditures are lessened, immense funds will be released into education and in a much smaller way, because of its close relation, into publishing. There is, too, the matter of current publishing activities conducted not only by the government but also by public or quasi-public bodies like universities, philanthropic foundations, and various national commissions. How such activities affect commercial publishing is ultimately relevant to both authors and readers.

It is probably axiomatic that in the twentieth century a nation must, to keep its pride, produce at home the basic textbooks for its school children. Such books are an obvious means of inculcating a spirit of patriotism. Shortly after World War II, a group of publishers from the United States visited several South American countries with a view toward finding new markets for their elementary school textbooks. They concluded that the opportunities were meager; and one of them later confessed his sympathy (which he assumed to be chastely democratic) with any country that refused to import "foreign" books to educate the young. More recently, John Diefenbaker while he was Prime Minister of Canada advanced a number of nationalistic measures, among these an appeal to Canadian schools to avoid if possible the use of textbooks produced in the United States. This kind of intense cultural nationalism appears somehow antiquated, and educated people in the contemporary world would perhaps like to excuse it as a lingering result of the rise of nations and of vernacular languages in the fifteenth and sixteenth centuries. The fact is that it stems largely from the second half of the nineteenth century, a period when, contradictorily, world-wide communication was first made possible. (We need to be reminded that historical phenomena are not always sequential. Many of the segregation laws in Washington, D.C., were not enacted in 1840 or 1870 but in 1910, which rather compromises the argument for "gradualism" in Negro-white relations.) Most governments have a political stake in public education and, by inference, in the books it employs. It is arguable whether a fundamental difference exists between the nationalizing of textbooks in Germany and France after 1870 and the tendency to follow a similar process in Canada a hundred years later. A difference exists, obviously, in the new-world aspect of Canadian education, which has still to teach basic language and citizenship to immigrants, and which still cannot be expected to depend —without some special pleading in textbooks—on a cultural tradition to permeate the training of youth in the natural course of events. (On the other hand, the problem arising from a kind of historical "lag" between the French- and English-speaking Canadians is not unrelated to the effects of a narrow nationalistic schooling.) In any event, jingoism is hardly the declared continuing interest of a democratic government in educational books. It has a more responsible interest in maintaining the scholastic quality and advancing the currency of those publications that influence the methods of teaching and learning.

For the British publisher, the spectacle of the national government actively promoting the development of particular textbooks (as well as other printed materials and audio-visual devices) would be less startling than it is to his American counterpart. Legislative commissions on education, or "white papers" emanating from the capital, are more characteristically British than American devices. Or, rather, this was a distinction that could have been made until recent years. Within the past five or six years, the American government has in part financed as well as largely initiated a number of definitive studies in the secondary teaching of physics, biology, foreign languages, elementary mathematics, and English. Most of these studies have projected the publication of textbooks and other printed materials. That this is a change in the government's view of education is obvious when one considers that from the Civil War until at least 1955, education was one of the few sectors of public life in which the power of the federal government had not radically increased.

In the past, whenever federal aid was given to schools and colleges it was carefully limited in nature, if not disguised. Money typically went for "free milk" programs in the schools, rather than for any purpose that would substantially affect curriculum or teaching methods. Except for the ceding of public lands in 1862 to colleges in the several states, practically no federal appropriations have been made to construct buildings, to pay teachers, or to purchase books. Such abstinence on the part of the national state, during a period when it was progressively expanding its powers, is owing to the tradition in the United States that local communities and state governments are properly responsible for the financing and control of public education. The tradition is strong still, but it is plainly under assault. There are contemporary demands on the schools and colleges that the states probably cannot meet by themselves: demands for accelerated learning in all disciplines (particularly in science) and social and political demands for greater educational opportunities for Negroes and other underprivileged peoples. Most politicians are now willing to admit direct federal aid to the schools. Legislative measures to accomplish this, however, are blocked by contention over the still-prevalent opinion that public funds cannot constitutionally be given to those schools that teach religion.

A part of this history is the stale and timid attitude of the American presidency toward education. Theodore Roosevelt was the last president to speak in highly personal terms on how education forms the national character, but he was regrettably more given to clichés than to ideas on this subject. There was little of the teacher left in Woodrow Wilson by the time he reached the White House (except as he dealt, didactically, with the truant nations at the Versailles Peace Conference). And the other intellectual president of modern times, John F. Kennedy, resorted to essentially unphilosophic proposals that would have the effect of loosing massive federal funds into education without setting academic standards for both teachers and learners. No new concepts on the reform of educational systems that date from a century ago have been advanced by the Commissioner of Education or the Secretary of Health, Education, and Welfare, who occupy weak and ineffectual sub-Cabinet and Cabinet posts. We have yet to find an American president who will risk political controversy by proposing the establishment of a national code to improve education and support the arts, and who recognizes the peculiar connection between the two in modern times.

If a kind of Napoleonic reform in education—which is what I am suggesting is needed now—does occur, it cannot but affect the publishing of both educational and general books drastically. The present-day entrance of the

United States government into education has already affected publishers in a number of ways. It has, for example, raised the issue of the privileges of publishers as private entrepreneurs. If public or quasi-public funds are used to create new textbook materials with the support of teachers throughout the country (as has happened in all these programs) then presumably that publisher who wins the contract to issue them has gained an advantage over other publishers, who are no less patriotic as taxpayers. Against this, it is argued that all publishers have the privilege of imitating such new materials and of drawing on them to improve books of their own, yet the fact is that many teachers are likely for some time to be partisan to the original government publications. If, on the other hand, it is proposed that publicly financed educational materials should be placed in the public domain immediately—and that no "official" publications should be issued—then the authors can reasonably complain that their efforts will tend to become diffused and will lose a certain authority. Government programs have, in fact, been handled both ways: the physics (PSSC), biology (BSCS), and language (A-LM) publications were awarded by contract to individual publishers, while the elementary mathematics study (SMSG) was put into the public domain.

This complicated issue could be better resolved, I think, if educators considered more seriously the role of the publisher in education. Ironically, even those university professors who were at first scornful of "textbook teaching," when they were recruited into these programs, bent their effort toward the preparation of new textbooks. One could have predicted this, for the book is a remarkable artifact: it demonstrates that ideas have been put into practice, and it is respectfully received. (Once, a committee of the American Council of Learned Societies was charged with the job of recommending practical means by which scholars could publish highly specialized works for their necessarily limited audiences. One of its conclusions was that the hard-bound book is not usually a suitable means, and that even letterpress printing is a luxury. The committee's report, of some ninety-two pages, was finally printed by letterpress as a hard-bound book on the grounds that in this way it would win the attention of university deans and presidents.) Indeed, one of the effects of the government's publications in elementary and secondary school disciplines has been to demonstrate how important textbooks (and related materials) are to contemporary teaching and learning.

If publishers were to be drawn into a dialogue on the resources and needs of contemporary education, one result may be a more sensible appraisal of the commonly repeated charge that they have a vested interest in standing against new ideas. During the past several years a spate of

books has advanced a devil's theory about educational
books as well as educational tests, notably E. Merrill
Root's *Brainwashing in the High Schools,* Arthur S. Trace,
Jr.'s *What Ivan Knows That Johnny Doesn't,* Martin
Mayer's *The Schools,* Banesh Hoffman's *The Tyranny of
Testing,* and James J. Lynch and Bertrand Evans's *High
School English Textbooks.* These have, with varying conviction, suggested that publishers wield a reactionary
influence, owing to their alleged predilection to cater to
the lowest level of competence among teachers as well as
to surrender to certain prejudices and social taboos held
by parents of school children. The consequence, it is said,
is books of compromised scholarship and a commonplace
style. That publishing is at times guilty of not only mediocre editing but also a craven and expedient mode of
selling should not be disputed. It will not do to be fatalistic
about crime, like the spokesman for the American Textbook Publishers Institute who declared that the schools
get the books they deserve. In the matter of public respect,
it is publishers who get what they deserve. This is often a
justifiable suspicion that they are more acute readers of
statements of profit and loss than of literature. In the
beginning, the publisher Kurt Wolff said, there was the
word, not the numeral.

A reasonable expectation is that publishing could
reform some of its own ills were it invited *on equal terms*
to discuss education with the schools and colleges. Such

dialogues really do not take place today, and one reason may be that educators are shy about admitting that they endorse the use of books that accommodate *present* conditions in the schools, while at the same time they criticize such books because they would not suit better, but still-unrealized, conditions. It should be plain, for example, that so long as schools allot meager funds for books (now about one per cent of school budgets in the United States), and so long as they expect, for reasons of economy, that students of widely divergent abilities and interests will use the same basic textbook in a particular course, then the books will reflect the weaknesses of any statement that attempts to say all things to all men. Moreover, the publisher cannot, like some of his critics, ignore the requirement that educational publications serve a *remedial* function. A reason that so many books are unsophisticated and overexplicit is that they are prepared with the realization that great numbers of teachers suffer professional inadequacies or incapacities. Nor have the schools been candid about the effects of the moral double standard in American life, a standard that permits young people to be exposed to liberal expression on social and artistic matters outside the classroom, but not within. It is presumed, for example, that publishers are deficient in taste because they omit certain works by important contemporary writers from anthologies of literature (not alone for secondary schools but also for beginning college courses). Yet the familiar double standard prevents textbooks from representing much of Hemingway (because of sexual description), Faulkner (sex again, but also passages possibly offensive to Negroes), Joyce (sex again, and anticlericalism), Baldwin (homosexuality, and passages possibly offensive to whites), and Orwell (references to Catholics, Jews, Protestants, and the middle class). For the time being, at least, no publisher has the authority, whatever the measure of his courage, to confront educators and parents with the issue of why anything goes on billboards and in the movies while practically nothing goes in school books. Perhaps it *is* a matter of authority. Interestingly, while no biology textbook had heretofore dared to illustrate the human *genitalia,* the publicly sponsored Biological Science Study Committee textbooks included such illustrations with very little demur on the part of teachers and parents.

Not too much should be presumed about either the liberality or the cogency of public officials, even those who count themselves educators. It would be dangerous to suggest that government agencies can, by the mere exercise of authority, improve the scope and nature of either educational or general books. There was, in 1960, the instructive example of the decision of an American school board to exclude Aldous Huxley's *Brave New World* and George Orwell's *Nineteen Eighty-four* from its high school curriculum. When asked about this, the Commissioner of Education of the United States at the time, Lawrence Derthick, said he had never heard of either book and therefore found it quite improper to comment on the action. Murray Kempton wrote: "Dr. Derthick was [earlier] crowned with an honorary degree as a Doctor of Humane Letters by Yeshiva University. In his acceptance speech, he expressed the gratitude of all scholars that his country was beginning to regain again that 'respect for the truly learned person that once so strongly characterized us as a nation.' Fortunately, for Dr. Derthick, this renaissance does not seem to have gone far enough to endanger his job." A local school official, who was a doctor in education, was reported by the press to have said, "I'm so involved in action that I never get to read much. . . . The last novel I read? I suppose it was James Hilton's *Lost Horizon,* but then I'd read that before." Kempton concludes: ". . . the last word on this belongs to Orwell. In his book on the Spanish War, he had a long section on a friend who had been put in prison by the Communists. It was a horrible story. Orwell, a tired man and a sick one, finished it with this sentence: 'It is ridiculous to get angry, but there is a stupid malignity in these things which does try one's patience.' "

The publisher cannot, obviously, depend on others reliably to defend books, and certainly not on public agencies. He cannot depend always on scholars and writers to use good judgment in this respect, and, most regrettably, he cannot even depend on his own profession. Shortly after World War II, the American firm of Macmillan turned over the rights to its book *Worlds in Collision,* by Immanuel Velikovsky, to the firm of Doubleday because, it was widely suggested, college professors in science objected to what they regarded as unwarranted assumptions and the method of inquiry in the book. Macmillan, with a considerable college textbook business, was presumably more vulnerable than Doubleday, which had none. And again, in 1963, Macmillan "withdrew" the book *J.F.K.: The Man and the Myth,* by Victor Lasky, after the assassination of the President. This hasty action ignored the fundamental position that if a book is worth publishing in the first place it can hardly be rendered disreputable and the object of suppression by a subsequent event; and the action was made even more bizarre when the publisher later "restored" this best-selling book to circulation but declared in a genteel fashion that its salesmen would merely inform booksellers that it was available but would not "sell" it. The fact is that publishers, in defining their relation to the public interest, must resist the tendency in contemporary society to condemn anything that is presumed to offend someone. The concept of tolerance in public life is cloying when it has the effect of compromising all issues. One is, at the same time, glad and sad that George Orwell did not live to observe such manifestations as that of a General Mills, Inc. directive (as reported by the New York *Times*) to the script-writers of one of the television programs it sponsored that they avoid giving offense "either directly or by inference to an organized minority group, lodge or other organization . . . college and school groups, labor groups, industrial, business and professional organizations, religious orders, civic clubs. . . ." The key word here is "organized." Freethinkers are on their own. And so, in the end, are publishers.

As part of the national experience, publishing's greatest, and more subtly enduring, engagement is with books of literature and scholarship. In the historical development of a national culture there is, however obscured at the time and however small in the long view, the presence of publishers. When Ralph Waldo Emerson called on the American Scholar to assert himself in his native voice, so that "the study of letters shall be no longer a name for pity, for doubt, and for sensual indulgence," there was a contemporary publisher who understood and was prepared to accept the charge. Of James T. Fields, the partner in Ticknor and Fields of Boston, his biographer W. S. Tyron says: "The role of Fields, indeed of any publisher, as an influence in the disseminating of culture has been much neglected by historians of literature. . . . Fields did not create the Augustan writers but he did create the market for their wares and thereby the acceptance of their ideas and the acknowledgement of their resulting fame. . . . Emerson called him the 'protector and guardian of us all.' " During a second renaissance of American letters, following World War I, a few young publishers were one of the catalysts of a new spirit in literature. The extent, and quality, of their participation in the rise of new writing in the 1920's is now beginning to be appreciated as there appear the biographies of leading novelists and poets of that period, among them Sinclair Lewis, Robert Frost, F. Scott Fitzgerald, and Thomas Wolfe. This is not, of course, a particularly American phenomenon. In Germany, the generation of writers whose best work was issued before the founding of the Third Reich was not only encouraged but also influenced by a few bold publishers, including Samuel Fischer, Ernst Rowohlt, and Kurt Wolff. And it would be impossible to write a definitive history of modern French letters without giving respectful attention to the brothers Gallimard. Even under the restrictions imposed upon contemporary Communist state-controlled publishing, a number of courageous editors in Poland and Yugoslavia have promoted a remarkably bold new literature in those countries.

From all this one might assume that if a small amount of good publishing is a good thing, then a lot more would be better, and that the government could bring about this result by making funds available for the publishing of books. With the assistance of the taxpayers' money, one might conjecture, the publisher would be able to assist the young writer he now turns away, to support the established writer and so save him from hack work, and to issue the important if also unprofitable works of the pedant and the divine. The results would, I think, be extremely doubtful. I confess to having declared too often (and, unlike Cato in the Senate, without result) that the publishing of more books does not ensure the circulation of more good books, and that the overpublication of books in the English language is seemingly unchecked by the hazardous financial conditions of commercial publishing. One cannot believe that in the United States and Great Britain, at least, any truly worthy book runs the risk of going unpublished. Publishers are not only engagingly eager to put into print any manuscript that bears the slightest mark of originality, but they are also foolishly addicted to the notion that a larger list will pay for an already too-great overhead. Nor can one say that, given a decently liberal opportunity to publish, writers are much the worse for having to compete for the publisher's choice, the critic's praise, and the public's attention. It is sentimental to suppose that important books can go wholly unnoticed. (Interestingly, playwrights are tough-minded in this respect. Voltaire maintained that if a play failed, the writer had no one to complain to but himself. It might help if novelists could be persuaded to this dictum, but admittedly only a sadist would force it upon the contemporary poet.) A case can be made, then, that a process of refinement of books takes place when writers must compete to draw upon the publisher's own limited resources. Yet this is hardly the only consideration involved in the use of "outside" money. There is the question of what does in fact happen when public and quasi-public monies are applied to book publishing, and how these might be better spent.

The most consistent and dependable publicly financed support for books comes from the universities, whose presses account for a sizable proportion of the books published in the United States—for example, almost ten per cent of the total number of titles issued in the year 1963. Their impressive position in publishing has been reached in a relatively short time; most of the university presses are less than forty years old, and the oldest, Cornell University Press, is less than a century old (1869) and has not, moreover, had a continuous life since its founding. (In the United States the "private" publisher is of older vintage than the university as a publisher. Lippincott began in 1792 as a bookseller, John Wiley in 1807, though English houses are, of course, older—Longmans was founded in 1724 and Murray in 1768.) There is no press in America remotely comparable to the Oxford University Press, which began in 1478 and is today the largest publishing house in Great Britain. Moreover, Oxford competes on equal terms with commercial publishers;

for instance, it issues textbooks and children's books and maintains overseas branches, as no American university press would conceive of doing. Oxford does not hesitate to publish "popular" trade books, nor does it generally suffer, like its American counterparts, from a sense of ambiguity over what a university press is supposed to do. American university presses, which do not pay taxes, like the commercial publisher, proudly accept the fact that they are nonprofit-making, though they stop short of making a virtue out of losing money, just as a commercial publisher would not admit to making money out of losing virtue.

No doubt the ambiguous role of the university press derives partly from its attempt to promote and sell rather specialized academic books through the same channels— book jobbers and bookstores—that carry the more popular works of commercial publishers. Works selected according to the limited prescriptions, not to say prejudices, of scholars can only be given a niggardly promotion by the university press, yet in the end this frustrates both the author and the publisher. An important function of the university press in the early days was to print the dissertations of doctoral candidates, a dreary business that has fortunately subsided during more recent years. (Until recently Columbia University required dissertations to be *printed* and was forced to create a separate press, the King's Crown, for this purpose.) There persists, however, the need to accommodate faculty members who write scholarly works under the pressure of that dread dictum "publish or perish," which is applied by many college deans and presidents to the promotion of instructors.

What is lacking in the support of the university press by the government and philanthropic foundations is a concurrent examination of those publications that cannot be initiated by commercial houses. One kind of project that is greatly needed is definitive editions of the works of American writers. A number of such editions are under way, but too few have as yet been commissioned and some, once started, have been allowed for lack of funds to lapse (for instance, the complete edition of Melville that was begun in 1947 by Professor Howard Vincent). A list of editions (compiled by Professor William M. Gibson, of New York University, and Professor Edwin H. Cady, of Indiana University) that *ought* to be published is formidable: Hawthorne, Poe, Whitman, Mark Twain, Melville, Emerson, Thoreau, Henry James, Cooper, Longfellow, Henry Adams, Howells, and Stephen Crane, not to mention twentieth-century writers of undoubted distinction. No commercial publisher is likely to undertake one of these projects; in fact, it is doubtful that he could, without a sizable loss of money, publish an edited and complete and reset edition of a modern master from his own list, for example, Ernest Hemingway or Sinclair Lewis. Scholars obtain grants from foundations to pay for part of their time as editors, but money is too rarely provided for publication costs. One of the annoying features of the modern profession of giving away money is that it repeatedly encourages scholars to write books that no one can undertake to publish and, if by chance published, no one will read. How much imagination is needed to move the national government to effect a concordat with several foundations and a number of publishers, including university presses, to publish the nation's great traditional literature?

Similarly, the only hope for what could be the greatest publishing venture of our time—and the one most needed by scholars and students—may be a collaboration between the government, the foundations, and both university presses and commercial publishers. This is an encyclopedia, a thoroughly contemporary encylopedia to which today's scholars and specialists would contribute under the editorial counsel that they write fully and freely with attention not only to accuracy and comprehensiveness but also to a readable style. Still another project in the public interest—or at least I have so ventured to call it in making the proposal to the American Council of Learned Societies—is a study of the humanities that would identify those particular fields that may be said to require research and criticism on the part of graduate students and teachers, *as well as those that do not.* There is no doubt that the graduate schools in the United States, perhaps still under the influence of nineteenth-century German scholarship, encourage research on certain subjects where none is needed, and in consequence writing is produced that is trivial and repetitive. Advanced scholarship in the humanities can readily become a kind of incestuous practice; it breeds within the academic family. Dr. Paul F. Brandwein was one of the initiators of a project for the Biological Sciences Curriculum Study that suggested to high school students a number of experiments on problems in biology that are still unsolved. This ingenious teaching scheme could, presumably, be adapted to scholarship in the humanities, and there is no reason why it could not be the work of a publisher in concert with academic associations and a foundation.

It would be querulous, and ungracious, to suggest that the modern foundation (Rockefeller, Ford, Bollingen, Guggenheim, Carnegie, Commonwealth, Twentieth Century Fund, etc., etc.) has ignored the public's need in the particular field of books. Bollingen *has* financed important publications, among them an edition of the complete works of Coleridge under the publishing direction of Rupert Hart-Davis. The Fund for the Republic financed the writing and, in some part, the publication of a series entitled *Communism in American Life* that someday will, I think, prevent the spread of a new myth, built upon the foundation of Senator Joseph McCarthy's old one, that there ever was a substantial adherence to Communist ideas in the United States. Yet the fact is that the boards of some foundations seem to have an inconstant view of publishing needs and are surprisingly ill-informed about the potentialities of the publishing business as a whole. Foundations are prone to speak of their aims, and those of society, in oracular and generalized terms, but, curiously, tend to commission works that are specialized and circumscribed. I think this results from a certain kind of blandness and professional urbanity that seems to be the mark of those who think in grand terms about the national interest. Walter Goodman, in reviewing a book by the head of the Carnegie Foundation, speaks of its being "the most *balanced* book I have ever read. Now, balance is the luxury of members of an in-group. It takes calm surroundings, security, freedom from distraction, a lot of confidence and a goodly amount of satisfaction with the world as it is to be able to see the pros and cons of every issue. . . . And it takes a remarkable faith in research and education—those pampered in-group industries—to be hopeful about us working out our dilemmas to an equitable and non-bloody ending."

What the foundations (with the exception of the Fund for the Republic) conspicuously have failed to do is to help publicize issues that cannot be satisfied by resorting to general statements of man's aspirations or the presumed eventualities of the democratic process. Public controversy is not, understandably, the goal of these foundations, but it cannot be a sign of bad management in them should it on occasion result from their publications. If books are the freest form of expression in most countries, then their importance to the work of public foundations is immense. Now that the number of magazines has declined—and now that those magazines that persist are less and less devoted to questions on which there is reasonable dissent—this may be the time for the book publishers to discuss with the foundations the feasibility of launching journals of opinion, or perhaps reviving the art of pamphlet publishing. (Some issues today are simply not engaged by newspapers. The New York *Times*'s handling of the response to Hannah Arendt's book on Adolf Eichmann, quite apart from the way it was first reviewed, suggests a typical failing of the contemporary press to examine *why* people dissent. Or again, the newspaper accounts of "the religious issue" during the 1960 presidential campaign were for the most part without relation to the question of religion itself. When Richard Nixon declared that so long as a candidate was religious his particular faith was of no consequence, no newspaper that I know of queried this unconstitutional and historically unsupportable position.) Yet it may be that I expect too much in this respect of an institution that depends upon the common consent, like a government agency or state university, or depends upon the public's grace, like a tax-exempt fund or foundation. Perhaps, after all, the publishing of the ideas of dissent should pay its own way—*that* is one way it can be refined and proven, as books of literary form and intent are now. And yet, and yet . . .

To publish is, of course, to make something known to the public. No part of publishing, whether its concern is with educational or general works, whether or not its financial support is wholly private, should be made safe from the common gaze or free from common criticism. One can hardly exaggerate the influence of books in the national history or their pertinence to the contemporary national experience. What one can do, and I suspect too many publishers are prone to it, is to be content that the importance of books is obvious, their continuance is assured, and their permanence is inevitable, when, actually, any work that relates to the public interest must be constantly reappraised. One needs to ask, currently and repeatedly, what the public interest is and what kind of publishing, among other forms of education and of the arts, will advance and enlighten it.

Index

Index

Index

Index

Polish publishing, 206

Pornography, 191. *See also* Censorship, Sex, in the novel

Press, American, decline of, 8–9; freedom of, 190–192

Prices, book, 21–22, 41

Principles of Psychology (James), 69

"Programing," 123–125

Psychological Corporation, The, 32

Publishers, as businessmen, 7–8; contradictions in the role of, 5–7; propensities of, 1–12; responsibilities of, 8–10; rewards of, 12

Publishing, and government, 190–208; and the public interest, 204–205; Anglo-U.S., 38–45; as "big business," 129–130; bad books and, 46; economics of, 4–5, 22–24, 58, 84–88, 127–129; eighteenth-century beginnings of, 85; English-language books and foreign publishers, 40–41; equations of, 87–88; excessive output of titles, 11–12, 14–15, 43; fastest-selling products of, 43; importance of, 8–10; international aspects of, 38–45; modest size as an industry, 14; relevancy of size of firm to sound publishing, 130; renaissance of in the 1920's, 206; role of in education, 199–202; staff needed for, 23–24; textbook, 22–25, 58, 116–129; "trade," 18–22; various types of, 13–34. *See also* Statistics, book, *and under names of countries.*

Radić, Stjepan, 147

Ranković, Alexander, 138, 148

Reading, as a private act, 51; teaching of, 35

Reference books, 16, 17, 26, 27–28, 32, 43. *See also* Dictionaries

"Remainders," 30, 127

Reprint publishing, 16–17, 28–32, 127. *See also* Paperbacks

Rich, James, 114

Riesman, David, 97

Rights, sale of. *See* Subsidiary rights

Roberts, Mrs. Paul, 124

Rockefeller, Governor Nelson A., 20–21

Romanticism, nineteenth-century, 91

Roosevelt, Theodore, 197

Root, E. Merrill, 200

Rowohlt, Ernst, 206

Ruark, Robert, 9

Sade, Marquis de, 93

Salesmen, book, 109–111, 119. *See also* Bookselling

Saroyan, William, 102

Sartre, Jean-Paul, 94

Schools, The (Mayer), 24, 200

Schroeder, Frank, 153